Morning Has Broken
Faith After October 7th

Yeshiva University
THE RABBI LORD JONATHAN SACKS-HERENSTEIN CENTER FOR VALUES AND LEADERSHIP

Toby

Erica Brown

MORNING HAS BROKEN

Faith After October 7th

The Rabbi Lord Jonathan Sacks-Herenstein Center
for Values and Leadership, Yeshiva University

The Toby Press

Morning Has Broken
Faith After October 7th

First Edition, 2024

The Toby Press LLC

POB 8531, New Milford, CT 06776–8531, USA
& POB 2455, London W1A 5WY, England
www.korenpub.com

© Erica Brown, 2024

The publication of this book was made possible through the generous support of The Jewish Book Trust.

All rights reserved. No part of this publication may be reproduced, stored in a retrieval system, or transmitted in any form or by any means, electronic, mechanical, photocopying or otherwise, without the prior permission of the publisher, except in the case of brief quotations embodied in critical articles or reviews.

ISBN 978-1-59264-683-8, *paperback*

Printed and bound in the United States

Dedicated to my mother-in-law

Barbara Brown

*who was hospitalized on October 7th
in Israel and died during this war,
and to nineteen-year-old IDF Sergeant Lavi Ghasi,
who was killed in Northern Gaza
and buried in the same cemetery an hour earlier.*

*And, finally, to Hersh.
How we hoped and prayed for your return.*

*May you all be remembered
for gentler, happier days.*

*In memory of everyone who was massacred
on that fateful day in October
and everyone who has died serving the country since.
And to the thousands of living heroes
who have not given up the fight.*

Debbie and Elliot Gibber and Family

Contents

Waking Up in Jerusalem   1
The Lord Is My Light   3
Morning Has Broken   12
The Soul's Surface Area   17
Raining on Mount Herzl   21
Painting the Dead   24
Walking Alone   28
Adulterated Joy   30
Giving Thanks   33
Letter to a Future Self   36
Shards of Light   38
Bending Toward the Light   41
The Maccabees Again   42
The Volcano   44
The Great Violation   47
Glorifying Martyrdom   49
The Dangerous Library   52
The Broken Myths of Childhood   55

Different Holiday, Same Message 59
The Situation Room 63
Fear All Evil 66
The Hive 69
My Cheese Drawer 70
Rebuilding 71
Exotic Mushrooms 74
No Excuses 76
Love Without Borders 79
Growing into Consciousness 82
Different Worlds 86
Dominant and Subordinate 88
A Mother's Love 91
Basic Training 92
Uncomplicated Love 93
The Gift of Particularism 95
Rethinking Social Justice 97
The Validation of Outsiders 102
A Better World 103
The First Protestor 105
Choosing Life 107
The Mountain Man 109
Blue and White 113
The Pause 116
Symbology 117
Say a Little Prayer 119
Protest Jewelry 122
Our Fault 125
The Long, Long Road 128

In Righteousness and Justice 130

A Theology of Distraction 133

Sitting Down with God 138

Sleep for the Weary 140

The Nursery 144

Rolling in Its Dust 145

Maya's Braid 148

Faith and Doubt 153

The Maternity Ward 156

One Day 158

The Last Normal Day 160

Regret 164

Blessed Is the Judge 171

Touchdown 179

The Soil 180

A Feather of Hope 183

Waiting 189

Our Library 191

The Windsurfer 193

The Saddest Day 195

In the Blink of an Eye 197

An Even Sadder Day 199

Stop Hiding 202

Praying in a Ruin 204

Getting Better to Get Worse 212

Sorry, Not Sorry 217

Jesters 222

Acknowledgments 227

Waking Up in Jerusalem

The sun cracks open on the city where three of my four children were born. These are God's hours. Silence shields the city. The world has yet to wake up. Soon the swifts will saw across the sky singing to Jerusalem. Then the sun will rise and bleach the city's walls. Here even the hard stones hold our fragile prayers.

"Jerusalem," Yehuda Amichai once wrote, "is a port city on the shore of eternity." At this hour, the serenity the psalmist prayed for seems almost possible.

The Talmud records that ten measures of beauty and suffering descended to the world. Jerusalem took nine and gave the world the rest.[1] Beauty and pain always live in proximity. Every woman knows that.

Whatever happens to this city and this country will elevate the heart and sometimes puncture it no matter where you live. Elsewhere Amichai writes, "Jerusalem is built on the vaulted foundations of a held-back scream."

These days, it is too often the scream of a siren as people in the south and north rush elderly parents and toddlers into protective rooms in ninety seconds. It's the Edvard Munch open mouth of young people from a music festival on the border of Gaza crammed into a bomb shelter when a grenade is thrown inside. It's the torment of a Jewish university student who is told to go back to the gas chambers, her belief in humanity splintered into glass shards. It's the mother who stands alone on the street crying and still waving goodbye to her son who left hours ago for his base.

The emotional shrapnel of trauma lodges deep inside the body.

It connects each Jew to the shrapnel of Jewish history. We are a horizontal people: suffering comes before us, and it will come after us. We are a vertical people, who hold onto faith and look heavenward at the meaning we attach to our pain and the strange way that suffering amplifies the contours of joys.

A few days ago, I left a wedding hall to watch a video of a hostage family. A few minutes later, I rejoined the dancing. It felt more honest to bring the suffering right there with me. Under the bridal canopy, we closed our eyes and sang, "If I forget thee, O Jerusalem…"

I cannot forget, even amidst crystal and flowers and young love. The verse mandates that Jerusalem is put above "my chief joy." To give a sliver of joy to the bitterness and a smattering of sadness to delight has taught us to live wholeheartedly in this short life. It enriches our faith.

There is always suffering on the way. There is always joy on the way.

It is good to be prepared.

The Lord Is My Light

> The Lord is my light and my help; whom should I fear? The Lord is the stronghold of my life, whom should I dread? When evil men assail me to devour my flesh, it is they, my foes and my enemies, who stumble and fall. Should an army besiege me, my heart would have no fear; should war beset me, still would I be confident. (Ps. 27:1–3)

The psalmist faces war unfazed. His faith is intact and carries him across the perils of battle like someone evacuated on a stretcher amidst gunfire. With God by his side, no army can induce terror in him. No one can intimidate him. The devouring of flesh does not unsettle him.

Each day of Elul I recite this psalm twice, but after October 7th, it unsettles me, so I deconstruct it, line by line, to see if it can bolster my faith during this war. Enemies *are* upon us. They *have* assailed us. The world looks away. Hostages waste away. Does the psalmist really have no fear? I am terribly afraid. I wonder what carries him across the narrow bridge of dread.

❧

It must be the small miracles of war that keep the psalmist steady. They are not small miracles at all. Today, on the 326th day of the war, my daughter tells me to look at the news; it's a small miracle. A fifty-two-year-old hostage, a Bedouin, Qaid Farhan al-Qadi, was rescued by an elite IDF unit from a tunnel in the southern Gaza Strip. Al-Qadi was abducted from a packing factory in Kibbutz Magen on October 7th. Ironically, he worked there as a guard. Today he will see his eleven children again.

※

Then there are the miracles of biblical proportion. One night in mid-April, Islamic Revolutionary Guards Corps partnered with Hezbollah and Yemenite Houthis to launch hundreds of drones, cruise missiles, and ballistic missiles at Israel. Almost nothing happened. Most Israelis slept through it and complained about school cancellations the next day. On a mid-August night a few months later, Israel preempted a retaliatory Hezbollah strike at 4:00 am aimed at decimating Israeli infrastructure at 5:00 am. Not one Israeli soldier died. The airport closed temporarily. Foreign airlines canceled flights. A few hours later, people went back to work. Flights resumed. That week, six hundred Americans made *aliya*. The brink of Armageddon dissolved into morning traffic.

※

"Many were the miracles You performed long ago, at night," we sing only once a year at the close of the first Seder. "Night after miraculous night draw near the day that will be neither day nor night. Highest One, make known that day is Yours and also night. Appoint watchmen for Your city all day long and all night. Light up like daylight the darkness of night." The white flame of rockets and their interceptors made night into day, and then the dawn arrived.

※

These are the miracles of this war that tighten my faith when it comes loose at the edges. Every time I divide into component parts a difficult event that jolts my belief, I find faith and gratitude in the pieces. Atomizing a miracle into more miracles is a Jewish strategy to protect what we treasure most.

Daily miracles, too, are my spiritual shield; they frame a melancholy day with piety and affirm my commitments. I consume them like candy, a bit of sweetness to dampen the sour taste of the news. "The words of a whisperer," I read in Proverbs, "are like delicious morsels; they go down into the inner parts of the body."[2]

Reliance on miracles, however, is not a military strategy. It can make us complacent.

※

It is this bedrock of faith that fortified the author of Psalm 27; his belief was there before battle so it would be there after battle. He was able to see God's hand through the worst because he had seen God's hand in his life through the best – before he saw the face of the enemy. The psalmist looked for God on the battlefield and then found God everywhere. The minor and major battle victories were stamped with God's outstretched arms. But then maybe the psalmist saw God in the losses, too. God hovered above the shoulders of an injured young soldier who carried the body of his bloody commander for miles until relief came.

※

Faith is harder for the unlucky ones, and there are, in this war, so many unlucky ones. The person who grabbed a last-minute ride to the Nova Festival for the weekend. Why not? The relatives who went to Kissufim for the holiday and did not come back.

※

My strength stumbles and falls, then rises high, then falls again. It oscillates. In every covenantal relationship, there are moments of distance and intimacy. I try to channel the psalmist to steady the pulse of faith.

※

Erica Brown

"One thing I ask of the Lord, only that do I seek: to live in the house of the Lord all the days of my life, to gaze upon the beauty of the Lord… He will shelter me in His pavilion on an evil day, grant me the protection of His tent, raise me high upon a rock" (Ps. 27:4–5).

☙

Through the haze of danger, the psalmist asks for only one thing: God's shelter.

In my mind, I outline the pastel painting on the concrete wall of a shelter I saw in Kfar Aza. It might have been a butterfly; it is covered in bullet holes.

That happy butterfly could not deceive nursery children from the shelter's function; those children in Kfar Aza were used to running into shelters. One grenade after another was thrown into those shelters. God will shelter us in His pavilion on an evil day, the psalmist promised. Just not on that day.

☙

"Do not subject me to the will of my foes, for false witnesses and unjust accusers have appeared against me" (Ps. 27:12).

☙

Ours is a history of unjust accusers. Do not subject me to the will of my foes, God. Their accusations spill out like daggers on pavement, clattering and threatening.

Sometimes our accusers have a point. They are not always wrong. Maybe we use too much force. Maybe we can only see our own suffering. Maybe we stopped caring about their children. Maybe we tolerate violent extremists in the government and radicals who set fire to their cars and villages. If we cannot stay human, we betray God. "Never once have I seen anything remotely resembling joy when we have killed terrorists," writes a reservist this year. "It's not an accomplishment, just a necessity."[3]

We do not listen even when the accusers speak the truth because they have accused us falsely so many times. We do not trust them. We defend ourselves instead. Golda knew. "When peace comes," she said, "we will perhaps in time be able to forgive the Arabs for killing our sons, but it will be harder for us to forgive them for having forced us to kill their sons." This killing hardens our hearts more than the twenty times that Pharaoh's heart was hardened in the Exodus. Wars are not won with soft hearts.

※

How soft is God's heart?

※

I wrote this book to articulate some of the struggles of faith that people have shared with me who are not living in Israel during this conflict. They feel both part of this war and apart from it. I wrote it in the first person because it felt more genuine to use my own voice and not speak for anyone else as I wonder out loud how soft God's heart is. It is hard to maintain a sacred heart in the throes of violence to my people and the devastation on all sides of this long, ugly war. I tried to write my way to that sacred heart.

I traveled to Israel four times during this past year. The first trip was two weeks after October 7th. The last was in August of 2024. I kept writing here and there and on the plane between here and there. I kept notes and lists almost daily. I am the child of a child survivor. Everything must be documented. We are charged to bear witness.

On these pages, I thread newspaper accounts and narratives from books on war into short passages that interpret Jewish texts through the lens of the current situation. Many in Israel have written and will write their eyewitness accounts. Fewer have considered how this war has changed Diaspora Jewry. I want to trace the internal weather I observed as we counted the days and offer fragments of anguish and hope over the course of one year of war on land and a continuous battle of faith inside the mind. Recency bias makes us forget the trajectory of the war and its phases. We are all victims of memory loss.

※

There are already dozens of books in Israel on the war: stories of released hostages, memoirs of soldiers, musings of parents and politicians. Outside of Israel, the war had a hold on Diaspora Jewry that came with immense heartache. The narrative abroad was laced with a different but related hate. This is a story that must also be told.

※

It seems at times that we are one family with an ocean between us. Love hovers over the water as God did at the beginning of creation. At other times, it seems like the Israeli part of this family denies us true entry. We are not entitled to dramatic feelings of loss and pain because we do not live in Israel, we who do not serve in its army or pay its taxes, financial or emotional.

Consider a visitor to the home of a mourner who cries more than the mourner while others look on at this vicarious display. Then again, we cannot judge the strength of anyone's feelings during war. Some people feel things more deeply regardless of where they live. Some live side by side with terror but don't allow vulnerability to seep in or leak out as one day blurs into the next.

※

Is it a blessing or a curse to feel things deeply?

※

Morning Has Broken

As I write this, Israel is still at war. It could easily be the fifty-ninth day or the 211th day. Or the 365th day. I mark the days throughout these essays in pursuit of a durable faith.

In the past twenty-five days alone, Israel has killed major architects of terror and what looks like most of a Hamas leadership organizational chart. I sit in the United States or in Jerusalem. The country anxiously awaits reprisals. The North of Israel is heating up. Hezbollah targeted the Druze town of Majdel Shams. Twelve children playing soccer were killed by explosives. There were threats and retaliation for the retaliation. It's hard to determine who started what. Maybe it doesn't even matter. Every side seeks a pretext for violence.

As one retaliation begets another, we rip off days from the calendar. One confident negotiator is optimistic. We are not fooled. We are tired and sad. We are saddened by the happy faces of soldiers, smiling into our eyes from the newspapers when they are already dead.

※

The negotiators' objectives are too grand and are, therefore, unrealistic: to achieve an end, to eradicate terror, to uphold democracy in the Middle East, to give a beleaguered stateless people their own home, to protect a people who spent two thousand years away from home. Right now, I'd settle for a normal day when so little happens that I am looking for something to do. I want to be bored.

※

"If your enemy falls, do not exult; if he trips, let your heart not rejoice" (Prov. 24:17). We cringe at October 7th's photos of Palestinian triumph. A shawarma joint called October 7th opened in Kerak, Jordan. In what world is a restaurant named after a massacre? "The date October 7th is an honorable date and will remain engraved in our hearts forever," said its owner when he caved to political pressure to change the name. "I am proud of myself and proud that I shook the fragile entity [Israel] by using the name of a shawarma restaurant and struck terror in their hearts…"[4] The cheering chipped away at our faith in the Other. We balk at the jubilant cries for an intifada on American campuses and lose faith in higher education.

But we believe in humanity and in higher education, so we continue the good fight.

⁂

One journalist claims Israel is actually in five wars, one to the South, one to the North, one metaphoric, and one ideological. The last war is internal: between progressive Jews in Israel and the Diaspora and those who are politically to the right.[5] Winning one war is no guarantee of victory in another.

⁂

> On Your behalf, my heart says: "Seek My face!" O Lord, I seek Your face. Do not hide Your face from me; do not thrust aside Your servant in anger; You have ever been my help. Do not forsake me, do not abandon me, O God, my deliverer. (Ps. 27:8–9)

I feel angry and confused, but I will continue to seek Your face the way I seek the face of my husband in an airport when he picks me up. My attention darts from person to person. That is not him. Is it him from the back? No. Then I see his familiar silhouette, and my body relaxes into a smile. The noise and movement of strangers gives way to comfort and belonging. That is what I seek in God's face. Comfort and belonging. And protection.

From October 7th until now, I find myself, often at dawn, asking how to think and act in this time of inhumanity. These musings are not chronological; they are products of a disordered mind during war, a period of hell I pray will never be repeated. They interweave classical Jewish sources and rituals with the events of the day because the haunting sense of oppression and battle fatigue trails me like a shadow from the beginning of time. I would rather bring my anger to God than hide it from God. A covenantal relationship demands that I bring to God the totality of myself.

><

"Look to the Lord; be strong and of good courage! O look to the Lord!" (Ps. 27:14).

Morning Has Broken

Hamas terrorists started this war early in the morning as they breached the barrier between Gaza and the Gaza Envelope. "Envelope" is a strange word, implying embrace, which is what these communities did. They embraced the border. Seventy thousand Israelis hugged the border of hatred that surged one October morning like a tsunami of devastation over a wall that was no longer a wall.

☙

Morning has broken. Mourning has broken. Morning is broken.

☙

"In the morning, you will say, 'Oh, that it were evening!' And in the evening, you will say, 'Oh, that it were morning!' because of the fear that terrifies your heart and because of the sight which your eyes see" (Deut. 28:67).

☙

That Simchat Torah morning, an officer in the reserves got a phone call. There was panic and danger and not enough military nearby. He grabbed his handgun and, as he left his Jerusalem neighborhood, thought of another crazy morning. He was seventeen and heading to school when he saw a school bus packed with children traveling to Yad Vashem. He hid among the bags on the back of the bus until the principal caught him missing school and angrily called the student's father. But how can you argue with a teenager who *wants* to visit a Holocaust museum?

The young man stood his ground. He would not take a taxi back to school. That day, he learned about Jewish suffering in concentration camps through images of devastation. He describes that morning as the beginning of his journey to Jewish identity.

Years later, this young man knew he had to drive into danger on October 7th. He stopped his car in the desert and walked to the burnt houses of Kibbutz Be'eri, thinking immediately about the chimneys of Auschwitz. In the light of the day, he entered the bleakest of nights. He wrestled a ceramic vest and a weapon from a dead man who had tried to defend the kibbutz.

෴

The strange thing about Holocaust museums is that they are designed to take visitors back to a space and time they never wanted to be in in the first place.

෴

When I was seventeen, I began my gap year in Israel. My mother came to visit, and I took her, a child survivor from a village in the south of Poland who was hidden in an orphanage in Lublin, to Yad Vashem. After a few minutes in a dark corridor limned with concentration camp photos, she asked to leave. There was a bench outside not far from an exit and, uncharacteristically, she lay flat on it in the hot Near Eastern sun for a long time. Behind her was a shining Jerusalem hilltop covered in apartment buildings and schools. Look, Mom, I wanted to say. There is so much new life behind you. Instead, I honored her pain and waited in the sunlight in silence.

෴

The reservist from Jerusalem, who had taken a handgun and a ceramic vest from a man who died defending the kibbutz, collapsed two mornings into one. Something was shifting inside him. "I feel that, as a nation, we are on the cusp of cultivating a new leadership and a new language. I believe our aspirations are greater than just a survival instinct." Survival alone is not enough. "I thought of my children, ages six and four, and I realized it was possible I might never see them again. If I did not survive, they would lose their father and a piece of themselves. But I also knew that they would preserve the identity and values that I was fighting for with my life."[6]

Faith is the belief that a new morning will eclipse the night. The belief that morning will follow night is an act of emotional resilience.

Day after day during this war, I have recited Psalm 130 alone and in community as I've waited for the morning after: "My soul waits for the Lord more than watchmen for the morning, more than watchmen for the morning." The refrain heightens the intensity of the waiting. A watchman's job is to wait for the morning when his shift ends. But our shift never ends because we must always stay vigilant. My friend tells me that her young daughters in a school in America now require a guard to move from school to the neighborhood park. What if someone sees that these children are Jewish? What if? Always – what if?

The lack of vigilance has caused endless misery. Sometimes we have to wait a long time for the morning. Sometimes it feels like the waiting will last forever.

The morning will come. I convince myself.

"O Lord, hear my voice in the morning" (Ps. 5:4). Before the world encroaches, the morning allows me to put yesterday's woes behind and entertain the possibility of newness. It allows me to fall in love with the world again and hope that God falls in love with us again: "Let me hear in the morning of your steadfast love," the psalmist prays (Ps. 143:8).

Even in Jeremiah's catalogue of doom, morning love blooms: "The steadfast love of the Lord never ceases; his mercies never come to an end. They are new every morning. Great is Your faithfulness" (Lam. 3:22–23). The morning revives my vigor and belief: "I will sing aloud of your steadfast love in the morning" (Ps. 59:16). This *chesed*, this steadfast love, makes sense in the morning. We regard the internal bruises of late-night arguments, even crises, differently in the tender haze of daybreak.

At night, one verse permits me to rest that's from another psalm I've said dozens of times this year: "See, the guardian of Israel neither sleeps nor slumbers" (Ps. 121:4). Danger lurks in the night. The time difference between Israel and the United States is a distancing mechanism that keeps Diaspora Jews slightly out of step with Israel. We wake up not knowing what has happened there for a few hours.

In three places, the sages of the Talmud ask, "Does God sleep?"[7] Lately, I've wondered if God is sleeping. Stay awake, I beg God, "when the Jewish people are in a state of suffering."

I am comforted by the words of my teacher, Rabbi Jonathan Sacks: Prayer, he wrote, "gives sacred space to the tears that otherwise would have nowhere to go."[8] Across the abyss, I reach out to God – the Guardian of Israel who neither sleeps nor slumbers. These are my very last words that put the distractions of the day to bed as I prepare for the darkness of night's uncertainty.

But significant events occur at the crack of dawn. Abraham saddled his donkey for the greatest challenge of his life (Gen. 19:27). Jacob rose from his ladder dream of angels and built an altar to God (Gen. 28:18). Moses built an altar at the bottom of Mount Sinai (Ex. 24:4), and gave the Ten Commandments a second time in the morning (Ex. 34:4). When Joshua was poised to cross the Jordan River and usher the Israelites to the Promised Land, he arose early in the morning (Josh. 3:1). In the days of the Judges, Gideon woke up early to test God's word (Judg. 6:38), and Hannah rose up early to worship God and beg for a son (I Sam. 1:19).

Every morning is like the very first morning.

The morning after this war, we will start living joyfully again, I reassure myself.

We are a morning people. Our faith is streaked in gold and pink across the heavens as dawn breaks. The sunrise looks beautiful even during catastrophes; in this broken world, a scrap of beauty always remains. Sometimes, even a skyful.

"Weeping may endure for the night, but joy comes in the morning" (Ps. 30:6).

The Soul's Surface Area

It is not clear what we will call this war, despite its official name: Swords of Iron. It sounds like the name of a bad comic book. Few in the Diaspora even know the name. I've never heard it used outside of the news. "The Simchat Torah War" would bind two emotional realities incongruously. It will ruin the holiday. Some have suggested the Second Independence War because we are undergoing a second, difficult birth of a new country. Some regard this as a continuation of the first Independence War with better ammunition and technology.

❧

Should we name a war because of its beginnings or its end? A name is important to pinpoint the collective mind of a people to a time and place. We can then say never again and almost mean it.

❧

We will each remember where we were when we heard about the massacre. A woman in the pew before me walked into synagogue late. She kept pointing to the word *"Yisrael"* in the prayerbook while staring at me. And then she said, "Israel is at war." Her son is a lone soldier, a term at once isolating and heroic. Her son was called up. He left a message.

Something terrible was about to happen, maybe was already happening. He did not know.

On Simchat Torah, we heard that fifteen or possibly thirty people had been taken hostage. We could not believe the number or understand how the border to Gaza stood undefended.

I could not dance. God, I love Your Torah, but I could not manufacture false happiness.

※

The number of hostages crept up alarmingly. The number swelled then contracted. Then it hovered. Then it changed. Now it is 251. As the fall turned into winter and then spring, we learned of hostages who died captive in a labyrinth of tunnels; some corpses were rescued. Five in one day. We watched the video of soldiers in their helmets and dirty uniforms say *Kaddish* at the place of discovery and thought we could not ever be sadder. And then we were. But people are not numbers. Someone tried to do that to us before. My grandparents' blue numbers faded over time, but I never – not once – thought of those remarkable people as numbers.

※

In Ben Gurion Airport two weeks after the war started, the woman handling the group's bags takes me in her arms and hugs me. She looks in my eyes in the loneliest airport in the world and says, "Thank you for coming" with no irony. I flinch. I am leaving in forty-eight hours. Weakly I say, "Thank you for staying."

※

When I put my passport into the identification machine, the first face that comes up is that of a hostage. And then the camera takes a photo of me. For a moment, it seems like our two photos live on top of one another. My fate is connected to his. But I am free.

≥

It's hard to be Jewish these days. It's hard to be human these days. The corridor to the baggage area in Ben Gurion Airport is lined with posters. It was an all-night flight. My eyes are tired, but that is not why I am crying.

I want to hold others up and carry them over the pain, but I can't. I can't carry myself over it. Because I can't, I want to travel deep into the pain so that I can tunnel to the other side of it.

≥

No act of barbarity surprises me anymore. Savagery disfigures me. This reality alone desecrates my humanity.

≥

In his introduction to Hannah Arendt's *On Lying and Politics*, David Bromwich writes, "The assimilation of the strange and monstrous to the familiar and tractable has an effect that goes deeper than politics. It cuts people off from their own experience. This *unexperiencing* relation to the world, in turn, makes them susceptible to further, stranger, more monstrous adaptations."[9]

October 7th is the assimilation of the strange and the monstrous. I cannot become a person who secretly believes that when only one soldier dies, it will be a good day. Then I become strange and monstrous.

≥

Many of our treasured assumptions about our neighbors have fragmented.

Thousands of miles away from the war, we are not in a physical war but in an identity war. Some of us know which side we're on in this war. Some are unsure. It doesn't matter. If you're Jewish, someone put you on a side and did not give you a choice. I remind myself that having agency means that you do have a choice of sides, even in wartime.

※

In war, we risk losing our souls to hate. Love is the small flame we cup our hands around so that it does not blow out in the winds of hate. I move with a candle, trying to get to a larger source of light before my own flame goes out.

※

In *Writing in the Dark*, Israeli novelist David Grossman warns us about fatigue during another war: "I feel the heavy price that I and the people around me pay for this prolonged state of war. Part of this price is a shrinking of our soul's surface area – those parts of us that touch the violent, ugly world outside – and a diminished ability and willingness to empathize at all with other people in pain."[10]

※

The soul has surface area.

Raining on Mount Herzl

Here, in beautiful, tired Jerusalem, I attend a funeral. Everyone these days goes to funerals, mostly the funerals of strangers because we are not strangers at all in the face of love or hate. We are *mishpacha*.

❧

Everyone knows someone who knows someone in this war. The longer the war, the more intimate we are with death and with each other. The circle tightens and strangles.

❧

In Jerusalem, it was bright every day on that first visit except for the few hours on Mount Herzl, the military cemetery, at the funeral of one of twelve soldiers killed the day before. It was spitting rain. Unprepared for the weather, I was underprepared for the emotional weather. The uniformed men of the dead soldier's platoon passed sandbags to each other for the dirt to cover the body in the grave. The body is not in a casket. It is wrapped in a tallit, the prayer shawl that inspired the Israeli flag.

I was not close enough to see. The rain intensified and the heavens poured down relentlessly. God is crying again.

❧

Staff Sergeant Lavi Lipshitz was a soldier in the Givati Brigade's reconnaissance unit. He was killed on October 31, 2023, along with Staff Sergeant Roie Wolf. Both were the first casualties after the IDF entered Gaza. Lavi was an accomplished photographer; almost every eulogy mentioned this about him.

Like many young Israeli men and women, Lavi left a note. It was for his sister Anafa on her computer in case he did not return from war. "I ask you not to sink into grief." He found grief exhausting and unproductive. No one asks for grief, Lavi. It finds us.

"Nothing is more difficult for me than idleness," he wrote, "so I ask everyone around me – always be doing something."

I'm trying, Lavi. I'm trying to keep myself busy so that I don't think about you too much even though we've never met.

❧

The mourners do not move even as the rain pummels them and their wet shirts cling to their chests and arms like second skins. They stand in respect and honor. Our group walks back to the bus passing older graves. I read the names on stones quickly and thank them each in a whisper. May God bless you and keep you wherever you are for paying the ultimate price so that Jews can live here in a mottled peace.

❧

Thank you, Lavi, for the wonder of your short life. It is unfair, so punishingly unfair. I do not know what to do with the injustice of it. I get back on the bus. We go to the hotel. We have lunch. I do not know how we can have lunch. I do not know how we cannot have lunch.

I know nothing.

On the bus, a seasoned rabbi guides us in reflection. He had never seen a grandmother eulogize a grandchild in all of his years officiating at funerals. The grandmother's voice was strong. She spoke directly to her grandson. Lavi, you called me every Friday to wish me a Shabbat Shalom. But last Friday, you did not call.

A woman walked out of the funeral sobbing and babbling inconsolably. Water. I need water. We put her on the bus. We get her water. We drive her to where she needs to go. You see, he was my student. Look at this photo of him. Here is a video. He was a photographer. He was always laughing. You see?

He is dead. No. We cannot see.

Painting the Dead

In a hotel with weak air-conditioning, a man in charge of the hostage crisis from Kibbutz Be'eri on the Gaza border asks us what we would do if ninety people we knew died on the same day. Ninety of his friends and neighbors died on October 7th. We bury our dead on the same day, but there are too many dead, he tells us. There were delays. There were too many dead to bury them all on the same day.

Thirty people from the kibbutz were also taken hostage on that same, terrible day. The lobby of the hotel in the resort area of the Dead Sea holds a table full of lit metal *yahrzeit* candles and decaying roses the color of old blood.

The wall is lined with posters of the kidnapped. It is a shrine to the memory of those dead and a visual prayer for the return of the living. Displaced children of the kibbutz now live and play in this scrim of land where Lot's wife turned back to Sodom and turned to salt.

In a few months, kibbutz members will return to the dining halls, assess the damage, decide if they will return. But initially none of these are options. A resort is only a resort if you want to be there.

❧

Children casually mill about the display of the dead. "Do you know anyone in these pictures?" a person in our group asks a girl of about four. "Yes." She points. "That's my grandmother," she says nonchalantly and then walks away.

In the same lobby, makeshift rooms have temporary walls, a table, and chairs for trauma therapists and the police to speak in semi-privacy with survivors. The therapists and the police try to piece together the details of the calamity and the confusion.

Each member of this kibbutz holds a narrative of tragedy: where they were, how long they fought, what the terrorists looked like in their black masks, how many they saw, who they saw gunned down.

They tell of how long they barricaded doors and who was murdered before their eyes. If they can speak. Each new story is an onion stabbed with a sharp knife that makes the eyes sting and the heart bleed.

One of the trauma therapists walks down the marble stairs with me and whispers, "A little girl saw an older woman crying while giving testimony. The girl told the woman to cry more quietly because she might be heard." These are the words of a child hidden and told to keep quiet lest a terrorist find her.

❧

When my mother was hidden by my grandmother during the Holocaust, she put her hand over my mother's mouth so that my mother would not reveal their hiding place. My grandmother reported that after a while my mother stopped talking. A child who does not cry for fear of drawing attention does not laugh either.

❧

An eight-year-old Israeli-Irish girl, Emily Hand, turned nine in a Gaza tunnel. When she was released, she could not speak in more than a whisper. Who knows when she will find her voice?

"I can't bear to think about what she's been through – she's been terrorized by terrorists in hell – but as her dad, it's my job to make it better, and I will," Thomas Hand tells the newspapers.

※

On the 199th day of the war, little Emily joins with the children of other hostage families in Hostage Square to sing *"Ma Nishtana"* on the first night of Passover. The song is captured on video. It could be the song of a youngest child anywhere on this night of the ancient exodus. Why is this night different? This night is different, Emily, because you are here.

Dorit Or dedicates the first cup of wine at this hostage Seder to represent Israel's exit from slavery to freedom:

"A first glass is dedicated at this time to the most basic freedom, which was taken from our friends who were kidnapped that Shabbat. Everyone has the freedom to live a full, safe and free life with their families, with their communities. Everyone has the right to be buried in their home soil."

Dorit's forty-nine-year-old son Dror was declared a hostage. His name means freedom. Dorit waited for news until May of 2024 when the IDF announced that Dror had actually died on October 7th with his wife Yonat. Two of their three children were released from captivity in November. Dror was a chef and a cheesemaker from Kibbutz Be'eri. Everyone has the right to be buried in their home soil. That's what your mother said before she knew you were dead.

Dror's body has not yet been returned. He has not yet been buried.

※

Further in the Dead Sea hotel lobby, a clutch of easels holds 8 x 11 photos of the dead next to black and white pencil drawings in various stages of completion. Kibbutz members draw someone they lost to hold on to a face, to suspend disbelief, and to draw the dead back into existence.

A mile away, on the beach, in front of the Dead Sea Mall, groups stage pop-up concerts, sports events, and group activities on the dark sand.

The haze that forms about the Dead Sea creates its own magical outline of calm. The sea looks alive. The people look dead. They shuffle past the same stores again and again.

Walking Alone

Back in New York, I fight off anxiety by walking. The crowd moves more quickly than I do. I do not see my pain on anyone else's face. I am solitary among the throngs.

The grainy image of a "kidnapped" poster has been shredded. Don't do that. These are my people.

※

I wake up to the news of a another *pigua* – a terrorist incident in Jerusalem – during the ceasefire. The fire does not cease. Three Israelis are dead. One young woman, an only daughter, was pregnant.

When Hamas stops, Hezbollah starts. South. North. Central Israel. It's a surround-sound of violence. Terror has no location. It terrorizes everywhere.

Am I allowed to say that it is hard to breathe?

※

War continues when we sleep. Panic ensues in the morning; my breath catches right before I pick up my phone. There is no space for any other miserable news on top of the war. Then we hear other terrible news, and the well of despair deepens.

※

I am a dual citizen, a divided self. My feet stand here. My heart stays there. I float in an ocean between, unmoored.

※

In my mind, I am a citizen of the world with global responsibilities. In my heart, I feel rejected from a world I was raised to embrace.

Adulterated Joy

Yesterday, shortly after I arrived for the second time, a single hostage was released. Another small miracle but a significant one for the family. On television, a broadcaster spontaneously snatches the yarmulka of a man sitting beside him and recites the blessing: *"Blessed are You Lord, Our God, King of the Universe who frees the imprisoned."*

❧

I have a late afternoon meal with a friend on Emek Refaim St. in Jerusalem, where German Templers once settled in the nineteenth century. Emek Refaim means valley of the ghosts. The dead always walk the streets with the living in Jerusalem. Her son is a soldier in Gaza. "Don't ask me my opinion on the hostages. I feel terrible, but I am the mother of a soldier who cannot complete his work because of the danger to the hostages. Why is someone else's son more important than my son?"

❧

Daniel Gordis, in his prescient analysis of the Abraham narratives, wrote that we would never sacrifice our children, no matter where the call came from. "But what would happen," he asks, "if we woke up one day and found ourselves in that very same land, and it suddenly dawned on us that even without knowing that we'd heard the call, we were actually sacrificing our children?"[11]

※

Fifty hostages were slated for release in groups beginning today in a complex exchange. Last night, the names and photos of the mothers and children were shared on the news. Alma Or is one of them. She's thirteen. Dror and Yonat's daughter. I've been wearing a pin with her face. Today, I will remove it and put it in a drawer. I woke up to learn that they're not being released today. The pin goes back on.

What anguish it must be to know hostages will be released, but your child is not one of them. Today is not the day.

What anguish it must be for a child to be released only to learn that both her parents were murdered.

※

We are glued to the news as Red Cross ambulances pass into a muted safety. The hostages were told to wave as if they were in a parade. Across the border, Israeli flags flutter. It's the same scene night after night, as if watching ambulances filled with hostages move slowly for many nights in a row is normal. A friend in Israel called it a mini-series. Every night we gather around the TV. Sometimes we wait for hours. It's a mini-series in purgatory where the plot is always the same.

※

I am addicted to what are called "emotional reunions" in the Israeli papers. It's the sudden bear hug of a brother reunited with a sister who cries into his chest. A woman has one arm around each child squeezing them both as hard as possible. That little Ohad running down the hospital corridor into his father's arms? I've watched it a dozen times, maybe more. It is joy but not joy. I don't have a word for it. I search the dictionary in my mind, but no word appears.

※

Every day, I force myself after I read some horrible article to watch a video of a makeshift wedding of soldiers or an offer of free hugs for those who are hurting. We rage against injustice. We take comfort in watching affection.

Giving Thanks

A month and a half of days pass. The newspaper offers Thanksgiving recipes. One boldface headline proposes a question: "Anxious About Your Turkey?"

Seriously? I'll give you something to be anxious about.

✥

I am in Jerusalem. Again. There are no turkeys in sight.

I write a list of what to be thankful for today despite the war. It's a decent list, but it's not long enough.

✥

We are grateful that we have an army to protect us. We didn't for most of Jewish history.

We are grateful that soldiers, many of them away for weeks without breaks, wake up each day and fight for democracy and Israel's right to exist.

We are grateful for those hostages who have been released and rescued and pray for them all to come home.

We are grateful that reservists everywhere came home to serve in the IDF.

We are grateful for the strength of those holding down the home front while their family members are at war.

We are grateful that Israel is more unified than ever.

We are grateful that Israelis put down signs of protest and responded to ferocious atrocity with unconditional altruism.

We are grateful for the everyday miracles of volunteers who are packing food, doing laundry, sorting donations, picking fruit, babysitting, driving, and attending the funerals of those they don't know.

We are grateful that Israel has a remarkable network and infrastructure of communal organizations in place that were ready and able to mobilize resources and respond quickly.

We are grateful that Jews across the globe are expressing solidarity with Israel when it matters most.

We are grateful that the rise in antisemitism has woken us up to the reality that we must show up for each other, now more than ever.

We are grateful that college students facing antisemitism on campus are finding the voice to fight back. This war will turn them into the future leaders of our people.

We are grateful that we have the technology to reach across the ocean in real time and support those who serve and those we love.

We are grateful that Israel continues to provide a sheltering embrace for refugees and immigrants who cannot live safely and securely elsewhere.

We are grateful that the American government and our allies the world over have supported our fight.

We are grateful for the many, many new babies born during this war whom we hope will one day enjoy peace.

We are grateful for the friends who carry us across the pain.

We are grateful for the love and support of strangers.

We are grateful that Israel continues to be the central and enduring project of the Jewish people.[12]

A mother cries into the phone, shaking her head when she learns that her daughter will be released. Crying ceaselessly is also a type of thanksgiving.

The two are reunited a day later. The young woman walks gingerly to her mother from the Red Cross transport bus and then speeds up as they get close. They fall into each other's arms and hug and wail.

Who is filming these intimate moments? Leave them alone. The mother crying into the phone. The daughter bawling on her mother's shoulder. Leave them alone.

Don't leave them alone. Please. I have seen too many pictures of horror. Give me something to hold on to so the torment recedes for a while.

Letter to a Future Self

One day far into the future, I will add personal details to the pages of Jewish history when I recollect this time for my grandchildren. Most Jewish stories, it seems, center on survival – the oscillating narratives of oppression, loss, resilience, and success.

⁂

We will experience the tyranny of oppression once more, and the cycle begins anew.

⁂

When those in the future ask me what I did in response to this crisis, what I say and do may be what they will say and do.

⁂

What will the future letter I write to myself contain so that I can live with myself when someone in the future asks? A Christian woman at the "March for Israel" rally in Washington, DC comforted a friend of mine, who was sobbing. She reached out to hold the Jewish woman's hand for a long time. This Christian woman traveled many, many hours to get to Washington. Why, the Jewish stranger wondered, would you come from so far away to be here?

"Listen," the Christian woman said, "I wasn't here for the Holocaust, but I am here now."

This Christian woman will be able to live with herself when someone in the future asks.

Shards of Light

The war stretches between Simchat Torah and Chanukah, touching and staining both holidays. It will tarnish other holidays in its wake, depending on how long it lasts. Sometime in the future, we will say to each other, "Do you remember the Chanukah of the war? I was…"

❧

The Six-Day War spoiled us into thinking a war could last less than a week if we were strong enough. But that is not the global norm. Most often, wars last so long that the rest of the world forgets about them and goes on to obsess about politics and sports and celebrities.

❧

On Chanukah, I try to be festive for the children even while my heart is breaking. I spin the dreidel, but whatever Hebrew letter it lands on, I already know we lost. We've lost people. We've lost trust. We've lost the stability that we took for granted.

❧

Cafés all over Israel sell ornamental donuts with lumps of powdered sugar or thick, colored glaze topped with jewels. How indulgent it is to eat such a pastry while a hostage eats rice day after day. But the baker also needs to eat. The child whose face is covered in sticky jelly also needs to celebrate a victory over an ancient oppressor.

⁂

The Talmud records that the most basic commandment of Chanukah is to light a candle each day per household. Those who are scrupulous will have candles lit for each person in the house each day. With each candle, the light in a home expands. With each person, the world's light expands.

⁂

I want to shout, "You can try to destroy us but know this: Every small spark will join another in the darkness." If there is any skill we have as a people, it is to keep a small flame going.

⁂

The rabbis in the Talmud ask a basic question, "What is Chanukah?" They answer with a brief historical synopsis. The Greeks entered the Temple and polluted the oil used to light the Menora. The Hasmoneans defeated the Greeks, entered the Temple, and found one jug of oil that miraculously lasted eight days. The Menora was once again lit. The rabbinic account downplays the military aspect of the story and focuses on the jug of oil. So much celebration for one puny miracle?

The rabbis understood that the military defeat was a miracle. Wars have their miracles. They also have their intense losses. But squeezing more than enough light out of what offers so little light represents our eternal contribution as a people.

⁂

Rabbi Jonathan Sacks, explains this small light.

> At the time, the Greeks were the world's greatest in many fields. They were unparalleled in their advances in art, in architecture, in literature, in drama, in philosophy. Even today, their achievements have never been surpassed. But Jews nonetheless believed, and surely history has borne this out, that there is within Judaism, within ancient Israel and still within its heritage today, something special. Something worth fighting for. Judaism, with its emphasis on the sanctification of life, and the belief that every human being was created in God's image, held eternal truths that we could not abandon. This was the unique distinction between the culture of the Greeks and the world of Torah and Judaism. As a result, Jews have always known that the real battle is not necessarily fought on the physical battlefield with physical weapons, but rather in the hearts and minds of future generations.[13]

Bending Toward the Light

On Chanukah, we light a menora in the window to show those passing by who we are and what we stand for.

We advertise the light as if it were for sale.

Mystics love light. Even in the darkness of the Middle Ages, they praised it.

> All around you – in every corner and on every side – is light. Turn to your right, and you will find shining lights; to your left, splendor, a radiant light. Between them, up above, the light of Presence. Surrounding that, the light of life. Above it all, a crown of light – crowning the aspirations of thought, illumining the paths of imagination, spreading the radiance of vision. The light is unfathomable and endless.[14]

The light is unfathomable.

The Maccabees Again

Weeks later, the count of dead soldiers from Lavi Lipshitz's city, Modi'in, is at twenty.

❧

Modi'in is the birthplace of the Maccabees.

The heroism of Modi'in continues.

Captain Eitan Oster, the first soldier announced dead when the IDF entered Lebanon on the eve of Rosh HaShana, was also from Modi'in.

❧

Mattathias and his sons challenged the ruling king of the Greeks, who insisted that all the Jews follow his rule and refrain from their religious practices.

Mattathias answered with a loud voice:

> Though all the nations that are under the king's dominion obey him and fall away everyone from the religion of their fathers

and give consent to his commandments: Yet will I and my sons and my brothers walk in the covenant of our fathers. God forbid that we should forsake the law and the ordinances. We will not hearken to the king's words, to go from our religion, either on the right hand, or the left.

How long do we have to give the same speech? Will there come a time when we stop telling those who subjugate us that we refuse to be subjugated?

※

Mattathias was about to die. He gathered his sons to give them a charge, "Now have pride and rebuke gotten strength, and the time of destruction, and the wrath of indignation: Now, therefore, my sons, be zealous for the law, and give your lives for the covenant of your fathers."

Walking in a covenant requires sacrifices.

※

Chanukah came and went. We stared at the small flames, hoping the light would grow and overwhelm us. But the flames did not magically turn into the sunbeams that penetrate grey skies in bad movies. It is still raining on the makeshift shelter where a soldier once lit a menora in Gaza. No one is there anymore.

The Volcano

At some universities, mostly coastal, Jewish students have been yelled at, spat at, called ugly names, hurt, and maimed on their way to classes. A student at an Ivy League tweets, "I think they are all dirty, dirty animals, they all deserve to die. They should be all exterminated. Just like Hitler did." The author also used language I am too embarrassed to put in print.

~

The normal reaction is revulsion. I feel revulsed. I also know that this kind of hate is extreme, and that most campuses are safe, and that we cannot magnify the views of extremists by giving them more attention than they deserve.

I also read these texts and try to quiet an abnormal reaction: the strange grammar police inside me. An entire police force lives inside my brain that wonders why students in these important institutions of higher learning do not capitalize, align their subjects with predicates, or punctuate properly. That's not the point, I tell myself. This is not the place to debate the merits of the Oxford comma. Tell the grammar police to give it a rest.

Morning Has Broken

※

Beautiful young minds have even been, in some instances, shamed and humiliated by their professors. A young friend in graduate school stopped going to class for her own safety. Her professor brought in a lecturer who said, "Zionists are just white supremacists who don't care about other people" in front of her. She was nervous to speak to classmates who might find out she is Jewish. In one class, she heard students celebrating and praising what happened on October 7th. Jewish clubs will not advertise where their events are taking place.

There is no tuition remission.

※

One senior in college tells me how alone she feels. This should have been her time.

The tentacles of Jew hate reach deep into every corner.

I've seen the statements and the texts of animosity, even and especially, from students in elite universities calling Jewish students out when all they were doing was trying to get an education.

※

Scratch just an inch below the surface and uncontainable disgust pours out like red-hot lava from a volcano that suddenly, unexpectedly, erupted. How else can I explain the volley of texts from another Ivy League student forum who called for violence: "If you see a Jewish 'person' on campus follow them home and slit their throats. Rats need to be eliminated from..."?

Nothing's been held back. The sick mind has too many platforms to broadcast untampered violence.

❦

Weeks later caution was advised. But it was too late. Violence was allowed to stream in every direction. The volcano spewed. So many precious souls have already been burnt from its heat. They are more fragile now. Melted and distorted in places, strong as rock in others.

I speak to a young man who found his tradition at a counter-protest. Another student has had enough. She decides to move to Israel right after graduation. This eruption has changed the trajectory of young lives.

❦

Volcanic eruptions are dangerous. They can be deadly. Clouds of boiling tephra rise from the top of the volcano and even its sides. These clouds of fire race down the mountain and destroy whatever is in their path. Ash falls like snow and blackens what it touches.

❦

Jewish students at some colleges have been called vermin. They have been told they are not worthy of life, and, therefore, have no place on campus. People call for the rape and murder of their fellow Jewish students without shame, not even a blush of embarrassment. Rape and murder. The same young feminists who speak out against date rape, and support a woman's right to choose, and demand that women not be objectified and sexualized are calling for rape. And murder.

It's a woman's right to fight back, they say, but they mean everybody but me.

❦

These rights are a categorical imperative. Consistency offers a more coherent narrative.

The Great Violation

A Hamas video from a kibbutz features terrorists torturing a pregnant woman and removing her fetus. Pelvic bones were broken on the bodies of dead women and girls. Mass rape was part of Hamas' plan. There are first-hand accounts of gang rapes. There is forensic evidence.

But this was not enough for Samantha Pearson, head of the campus sexual assault center at the University of Alberta in Edmonton, Canada. She signed a letter denying that terrorists raped Israeli women and girls on October 7th. She who was not there. Her body is intact. There is no tenderness, no sympathy, no willingness to believe what has been documented with facts. She lost her job, but the splinters of her vitriol stay.

※

This is the failure of selective feminism.

※

Rape has been justified as a valid tool for freedom fighters. Can rape ever be justified, especially by a woman? Someone posted their disgust: "Shouldn't a sexual assault center believe all victims, and not just the non-Jewish ones?" If a rape victim's testimony is not believed, there is little point in a sexual assault center.

※

Ask a woman if she would rather die or be raped, and she might hesitate for a brief second. Rape is the violation of all violations on the body and on the mind. I don't know if men live with the fear of rape. I don't know a woman who doesn't.

Rape victims live with shame, degradation, and the punishing reliving of the act that death would have taken away. The inside of a person has been stolen and replaced with nightmares.

Rape is like dying again and again and again.

Glorifying Martyrdom

I am disoriented.

Administrators dismiss the posts calling for Jewish extinction and the death of Israel as exaggerations. That does not represent "our community," the university president says. Open your eyes. Glorifying martyrdom in big letters and advertising the elimination of Jews and Israel "from the river to the sea" on the side of a university's façade does not represent an administration. This is true. But it is insufficient. It represents the voice of students vocal enough to stir up support for a cause that calls for the destruction of other students.

⁂

I've always believed that education is a slow process of confirming facts and interrogating previously held beliefs. The classroom should be secure enough to confront every intellectual demon.

⁂

Freedom of speech creates discomfort. Hate speech that incites violence, racism, antisemitism, or anti-Islamic sentiments is a crime. The behavior of criminals is a punishable offense.

Killing an innocent man in Los Angeles who is standing at a protest is a crime.

※

Almost exactly five years ago, a murderer attacked the Tree of Life Synagogue, and on American soil, butchered eleven people. We were shocked then.

※

The weak statements made by educational institutions is alarming. I will not forget the anemic documents of ethical equivalence by college presidents in this hour. In the best-case scenario, someone from the communications office revised the statement a week or two later to sound less ambiguous. This was not out of principle. A principled response would have worked the first time.

Alumni, parents, and donors put pressure on college administrations. The backtracking of college presidents smelled of money.

※

The failure to acknowledge terrorism is a failure to understand the root of this war, but, more importantly, for American higher education, it represents a failure of leadership. In Maslow's hierarchy of needs, security is at the base of the pyramid. The most basic role of a college president, administration, and faculty is to protect the safety of *all* students.

※

The prestige and the tuition of many universities today pales in comparison to the preservation of a Jewish student's dignity and self-worth.

※

A college president, no matter how straight his or her moral spine does not share a student's college experience. A college president does not live in a dorm, go to classes, eat in the cafeteria, or hang out on the quad. The nicest office on campus is unlikely to bring deliverance.

The Dangerous Library

When I was in elementary school, I spent most lunch periods and recess in the library with Mrs. Blank. She was the librarian who looked like a caricature of a librarian, with her grey ponytail and her glasses and her sensible black pumps. Mrs. Blank always looked at me with merciful eyes. She knew I loved reading, but that's not why I was in the library. She also knew I was avoiding bullies, who tend not to hang out in libraries. They were ugly, those bullies who made me do their homework, took anything good out of my lunch, and made fun of my clothes.

The books were my refuge. Like Mrs. Blank, they were quiet and kind. They didn't scream or throw things. Their pages felt sturdy and solid and smelled like armor.

✥

A young friend was trapped in a library of a university in the fall not long after October 7th because a mob was shouting wildly and pounding at the entrance. If I close my eyes when I play the video, it is the sound of animals at the door. In a place of higher learning.

For forty minutes, no security showed up. A small group of engineering students could not handle this on their own. I saw them frozen in fear.

Morning Has Broken

❧

This was not supposed to happen in a library. A library is supposed to be the safest place on earth.

❧

There is something slow, unrushed and generous about libraries. Ideas stand quietly like soldiers in the stacks. Universes open there. Everything in that cathedral of knowledge and imagination is mine for the taking. It is in the library where I travel as I sit. The page transports me far away, and I abandon time in the pleasure of words and the meditative turning of pages; I love the smell of old books whose jacket covers sound like crinkled cellophane.

❧

I love libraries, and I hate hate, so I wrote to the president of that university. I know that young woman, and I was afraid for her. I cannot unsee that mob or unhear their violent drumming on the doors. That young, budding engineer will go back to class wondering who in the room hates her without even knowing her.

❧

Dear President,

This must be a difficult time for you, and I send my commiserations. There is so much to process about higher education in this moment.

I am reaching out to you as someone who taught a weekly class at your university to students decades ago when I was a student myself.

I write to you as someone who deeply admires the graduates from your university I have interacted with over the years.

I reach out to you as a higher education administrator in the same city.

I reach out to you as the mother of a close friend of one young woman who was in your library yesterday. That student is deeply shaken by the pounding on the doors that told her Jewish lives were at risk in your library. Can you please respond to my twenty-two-year-old daughter who called home in tears last night asking why so many people on college campuses hate Jews? Can you repair the visceral fear she and her friends are experiencing in this moment and tell her in full confidence that she is safe?

I write to you as a parent who does not understand why it took so long to protect these students when without protection our children cannot study. As you know better than anyone, where anxiety lives, learning cannot live.

I write to you as a person who taught "Diversity and Inclusion" in a graduate school for five years. Now I watch university DEI committees abandon Jewish students in the name of an intersectionality that glibly divides people as oppressed or oppressors and ignores antisemitism as the only microaggression that is tolerated.

I write to you as the child and grandchild of Holocaust survivors who never thought I would witness the barbarity of the October 7th massacre and kidnapping of babies and the elderly.

I write to you as an educator who questions what we are teaching in university today if graduates leave with a diploma but a broken moral compass.

I write to you as a dual citizen of Israel and America who values democracy.

I write to you as a Jew who is suffering.

I write to you as a human being who is in pain.

I write to you because to do nothing in this moment is to give life to hate.

I got no response. Not even an automated one. Not even a bad one.

The Broken Myths of Childhood

When my youngest child called home that day of the library lockdown, she was crying the breathless type of tears that no parent ever wants to hear. Why, she wanted to know, do people hate Jews so much?

I wondered when that realization would come to her with apprehension's totality. It is a sad day when the comforting myths of childhood die.

※

In every generation, the hate for Jews morphs, I explained, but it does not go away. Like a virus, it waits for the moment to break forth and destroy. The difference is that hate does not die then. Babies of the next generation are born with it because hate is from the home and in the milk of nursing mothers and hateful fathers. And it will wait inside that baby and grow as that baby grows.

※

My daughter was not asking a factual question. She knew about antisemitism in our history because it dominated my family's Holocaust narrative. But her life was blessedly free of it. When it comes to knowledge, there are cognitive understandings and emotional realizations. They are not the same thing. One hits harder than the other. One elevates the mind. The other crushes the soul. Knowing that someone hates her just because of her faith without ever knowing her is a great injustice.

The moment I realized that some people hate me for existing destroyed my pure view of the world. That fiend came for my daughter. And for her siblings. And her father. And for her grandparents and their parents. It's a tradition, you might say, a menacing understanding of the world passed down from one Jewish generation to the next.

❧

She read about Jew-hate in fiction, history, and memoirs. She visited concentration camps in Poland. But then she saw her friend stuck in that library and realized that antisemitism always seems like someone else's story from a long time ago until that day when it comes for you or someone you love. Then it becomes more real than anyone else's fact.

❧

When I was a teenager, I was annoyed at my grandparents' constant suspicion. It seemed like everyone was an antisemite until proven otherwise. I rebuked them for overreacting. The world already reached the lowest level of hell. There is nowhere to go but up. It can't happen again. We've learned from this huge and colossal mistake. Don't be so paranoid. "We already had antisemitism," I said as if it were a common cold that just went away.

❧

"I'm sorry, Bubbie and Zeide," I yell to your graves. I love you so much. I was so wrong.

❧

Antisemitism, according to reliable reports, is up by almost 400 percent in the United States and more than double that in parts of Europe. Jewish institutions have been vandalized. *The Guardian* reported over a thousand acts of antisemitism in the U.K. since October 7th, all in less than one month. More than sixty of those hate acts were directed at schools and schoolchildren. In the fourteenth arrondissement of Paris, blue stars of David were stenciled on multiple buildings, possibly targeting Jews in those buildings. Just an hour ago, the news reported that notes were left on cars at a Chicago park that read "9/11 was a Jewish job" and other hateful slogans. Israel's president holds up a copy of *Mein Kampf* praised by Hamas as a guiding tract of their movement.

⁂

This is probably the first time students have suffered consequences in America for a war in Israel. I am worried for them. Things are different in war. Our days seem harried and different. The mind is such a fragile thing. They may be wounded by the constant news of assaults on our people. They may wonder if some classmates want them to die the way Hamas wants every Israeli dead. They may harbor my grandparents' old suspicions and now walk with a smaller footprint.

⁂

A new friend, a senior in college, told me that her progressive non-Jewish friends reached out to her with compassion right after October 7th. Then, a few days later, she saw a video of a protest on campus; one of her friends was front and center. The flag was waving high. Glory to martyrs.

She asked for a meeting. Crying, she told him that "from the river to the sea" is a call for the elimination of Israel. It calls for the destruction of her people and the only land that is her refuge if the worst of Jewish history repeats itself. He had no idea what that slogan meant. He did not know what river. He did not know what sea. He waved the flag because that's what everyone else was doing. He was supporting the underdog. He shows up for the underdog.

Listening to her, he must have suddenly realized all he did not know.

Peggy Noonan wrote that when she was a college student during the Vietnam War, the mantra was "Don't trust anyone over 70." Today, it is "Don't trust anyone under 30."[15]

On October 8, I said to a friend, "Look, the world is with us." He said, "Wait until tomorrow."

Different Holiday, Same Message

Long grey sheets of rain bucketed down the Shabbat of *Zakhor* – when we recite verses to fulfill the mitzva of remembering the biblical Amalekites. The synagogue is packed. Neon orange rain ponchos lie draped over folding chairs. There is a lot of friendly banter; neighbors are happy to see each other and share their stories of battling the morning's storm.

> *Remember what Amalek did to you on your journey, after you left Egypt – how, undeterred by fear of God, he surprised you on the march, when you were famished and weary, and cut down all the stragglers in your rear. Therefore, when your God grants you safety from all your enemies around you, in the land that your God is giving you as a hereditary portion, you shall blot out the memory of Amalek from under heaven. Do not forget!* (Deut. 25:17–19)

We will not forget how you destroyed the stragglers: the famished and the weak. We recall how one tribe tormented us and their descendants – united genetically by the DNA of violence – are still here. We blot out their memory, which actually means we will never blot out their memory.

❦

It's Purim. Day #170 of the war. Two hundred fifty-two soldiers have died. There are over 130 hostages still in Gaza. The first two numbers are exact. The third is not. The inherent condition of captivity is uncertainty.

❦

My husband is reading an abbreviated version of the book of Esther to our oldest grandson on the couch. "And then Haman decided to kill all the Jews…" At five, our grandson is inducted into the story of hate. We don't even think twice about this fact of our existence. It's in a children's book. When we don't want children to hear difficult realities of the adult world, we whisper, tell half-truths, lie, whitewash, spell the words, or avoid speaking altogether. But this hate of our people we speak out loud as if it were the most natural thing in the world.

❦

The same grandson sneaks into my bed about an hour before the sun rises, "I'm so excited. I'm going to have billions of junk."

❦

By the end of Purim, the kitchen table is a mountain of Hershey kisses, stale licorice, and tangerines. I promise myself I won't eat any of the hamantaschen – unless they have apricot filling.

❦

Mordechai, in chapter nine of the book of Esther, mandated the way the war was to be remembered. He recorded the events and then declared ritual observances. Each mitzva of Purim corresponds to and addresses a different challenge of war and offers four prescriptions to neutralize hate's traumatizing effects. Chronicling the account and hearing the scroll involves controlling our own narrative and sharing it. Having a festive meal creates a pause to reset the human condition to joy. We are good at meals to commemorate near destruction. Bestowing gifts to friends contrasts with suffering the brutality of enemies. Giving charity reopens the magnanimity of abundance that diminishes in times of war. We respond to unconditional hate with unconditional love. *Matanot ketanot*. Small gifts. One way we combat evil is to fight. Another way is with generosity.

※

Each commandment responds to, commemorates, and heals the wounds of war, both then and now. Mordechai, in an act of leadership genius, understood what was needed in the moment and in perpetuity.

※

The IDF releases its report on Kibbutz Be'eri. It's comprehensive and devastating. Minute by minute, hour by hour, it records the assault and how unfortified and unprepared the kibbutz was for the onslaught. I say to my husband, "But no one could have known. This never happened before" as if defending the lack of security. He replies, "It's on Gaza's border. It's not a surprise. We should have been prepared."

※

I listen to a reporter analyze the Be'eri findings as I walk the long corridor of an American airport. So many kibbutzniks were locked in safe rooms for hours until help arrived while terror reigned outside. A man in front of me wears a black T-shirt that says "Don't Let the Hard Days Win" on the back. The hard days won.

※

In the book of Esther, Haman decided that Mordechai and his entire people should be punished because Mordechai refused to bow down to him. Haman confided to Ahasuerus, "There is a certain people, scattered and dispersed among the other peoples in all the provinces of your realm, whose laws are different from those of any other people and who do not obey the king's laws; and it is not in Your Majesty's interest to tolerate them" (Est. 3:8).

The message is as old as time. People who are different are not to be tolerated. Jews were an easy target. Haman was guilty of wanting the king's job, so he made the Jews guilty of disobeying the king.

Not tolerating people should not mean killing them: "If it please Your Majesty, let an edict be drawn for their destruction, and I will pay ten thousand talents of silver to the stewards for deposit in the royal treasury" (Est. 3:9). Haman paid for the right to annihilate the Jews. "Thereupon the king removed his signet ring from his hand and gave it to Haman son of Hammedatha the Agagite, the foe of the Jews" (Est. 3:10).

It was that simple. The twist of a ring determined the fate of an entire people.

No more explanation was necessary. "And the king said, 'The money and the people are yours to do with as you see fit'" (Est. 3:11). Ahasuerus washed his hands of guilt.

Was the king concerned that destroying one people among his 127 provinces would create an avalanche of political insecurity for everyone else? Apparently not.

꘎

Antisemitism is not a Jewish problem where only the victims need be concerned. It's a societal disease that needs to be extricated at its root. Hamas is not a Jewish problem. Hezbollah is not a Jewish problem. Their hatred of the West is a rejection of the values I was nourished on. This begins with Israel but will not end with Israel. It never does.

The Situation Room

In Jerusalem, I visit a *chamal* – a *cheder milchama* or situation room that's been set up a few blocks from the city's central shopping area. It's not really a war room, though. It's a warren of rooms where volunteers come to organize efforts.

Thousands of volunteers have passed through these halls. One room is set up for security and technology. One room is filled with groceries, toilet paper, and cleaning products. One room has professionals on phones providing free therapy. There is a "store" where evacuees from the fifty-five hotels hosting them in Jerusalem come to get clothing and toys. Everything is free, but it resembles a store to dignify the shoppers who left their homes with the panic and rush of those who could think only minutes ahead. There are between thirty thousand and thirty-five thousand evacuees here to dress and feed.

There is surplus of kindness everywhere I look. The space buzzes with vitality. But all the evacuees just want to go home.

※

Love here is free for the taking. Unconditional love is loving someone just for existing. It's the only cure for hating someone just for existing.

❧

Everywhere in Israel, people are feeding and clothing soldiers, babysitting for the children of widows, and doing the laundry of evacuees as if it were their own. It's hard to have strangers launder your intimate things for over forty days. Maybe their white socks will turn pink under your care. But the washing is done with meaningful intent. But for the grace of God go those with washing machines and dryers. Scrub and scrub away the hate, the blood, and the dirt.

❧

During the summer of 2023, Israel seemed to be on the brink of a civil war straight out of the book of Judges. But now, many of the same networks used to organize massive protests are expediting networks of giving. The energy of anger morphed into the buoyancy of benevolence. Volunteers on both sides of the judicial reform argument packed cans of vegetables side by side. There will be time to pick up the picket signs soon enough. For now, volunteers share small talk and tears.

❧

Have your bags been with you the whole time? Did you pack them yourself? You know why I'm asking. She speaks in halting English. I must have answered these questions a hundred times before. But today my answer is not the same. No, actually. I was given these two duffle bags of boots by a stranger from a synagogue not far from the airport who heard that a platoon needed boots. Each boot has been sized for a specific soldier. I think they've already sent about a thousand pairs. Don't worry. I tell her. They're only boots. Check for yourself.

❧

In the United States and elsewhere, we send money, clothes, and protective gear. Sometimes we send too much shampoo to soldiers who don't have much hair, but we do it because we must do something. Lavi

Lipshitz told us to keep busy. We channel our anxiety into duffle bags to chase away the fear. Let a stranger across an ocean open a suitcase, lift out a token of altruism, and hold on to human goodness for an hour. We buy and send the way a mother presses food on children who are not hungry.

❧

Here we worry and give. There they worry and give.

❧

When the war is over – may it be soon – the poor, the sick, the frail, and the homeless will still be both here and there wondering where all the volunteers have gone.

Fear All Evil

"Fear no evil," the Bible says (Ps. 23:4). I fear evil. I fear it a great deal these days. I also fear that we are not quick to name evil anymore.

❧

Evil is a biblical word. The naming and imprint of evil is all over the Hebrew Bible.

"I hate pride and arrogance, evil behavior and perverse speech," we read in Proverbs (8:13).

Some people can't get enough of it: "For they cannot rest until they do evil; they are robbed of sleep till they make someone stumble" (Prov. 4:16).

Job complains about it. "As I have observed, those who plow evil and those who sow trouble reap it" (4:8).

"Woe to those who call evil good and good evil," says Isaiah, "who put darkness for light and light for darkness, who put bitter for sweet and sweet for bitter" (5:20).

Morning Has Broken

Evil in authority figures is particularly detestable: "God sent a message to King Jeroboam: 'You have acted with more evil than all those who preceded you...'" (I Kings 14:9).

❦

I hold onto the redemptive thread of the prophet Samuel, "Do not be afraid," Samuel replied. "You have done all this evil; yet do not turn away from the Lord. Serve the Lord with all your heart" (I Sam. 12:20). We still have a chance.

❦

When I am mentally overstretched from fearing evil, I turn to one of my heroes, Natan Sharansky, who was confined in prison for many years but never let anyone else own his mind. "Over the years," he wrote, "I have come to understand a critical difference between the world of fear and the world of freedom. In the former, the primary challenge is finding the strength to confront evil. In the latter, the primary challenge is finding the moral clarity to see evil."[16]

❦

In these long days of moral relativism, the failure to recognize and label evil is the sign of a liberal ethos riddled with dysfunction. To admit to the persistence of evil is to take, in part, responsibility for it. It is a confession of wrongdoing that obligates.

This is why I feel so grateful when a non-Jew fights against evil perpetrated toward Jews or when a Jew fights racism or anti-Muslim hatred. Victims should not be the only or the primary protestors against the abuse they sustain. When I can, I embrace, praise, and thank that person. It's a modern-day miracle. It must be a basic function of being human to call out evil and work toward its elimination. I expect it of myself. I should not be surprised to find it in others.

❧

"People," writes Kwame Anthony Appiah in *Cosmopolitanism: Ethics in a World of Strangers*, "often recommend relativism because they think it will lead to tolerance. But if we cannot learn from one another what it is right to think and feel and do, then conversation between us will be pointless. Relativism of that sort isn't a way to encourage conversation; it's just a reason to fall silent."[17]

❧

"The evil that a man does is never done under false pretenses..." writes the nineteenth-century German scholar Rabbi Samson Raphael Hirsch.[18] When people say they are going to destroy us, we must believe them.

❧

Growing up, we read about Joseph Stalin, Adolf Hitler, Pol Pot, Ivan the Terrible, Idi Amin, Saddam Hussein, and Osama Bin Laden. Their evil did so much damage before they were stopped. Looking back at history, I find myself questioning why it took so long to stop them. Looking at the news, I understand. We do not know the extent of the wreckage until it's over, and the reign of terror ends. The dead become a tally for history's accounts. History books list; they do not apologize.

❧

Hassan Nasrallah is dead. There is celebration on the streets of Syria.

The Hive

Naming evil also means interrogating my own tribalism and when it interferes with good judgment. It is why we were told in Deuteronomy to put courts of justice in every city. We have to regulate ourselves.

Jonathan Haidt argues that sometimes we can set individualism aside to work like bees in a hive, dedicating ourselves to the good of the group. These are times I cherish. "Our bee-like nature facilitates altruism, heroism, war, and genocide." But Haidt warns that our "hivishness" can blind us to looking critically at ourselves. We bind ourselves into groups and once we pick "a particular narrative" we blind ourselves from seeing alternate moral worlds.[19] Our moral frameworks bind and blind.

I worry that we risk willfully blinding ourselves to civilian deaths and, in so doing, warp our hearts. We cannot label everyone a terrorist. But civilians are not necessarily only civilians. We have learned that in this war. The rot of suspicion afflicts the faithful. In war, we can make the enemy invisible. In religion, we cannot. If we want to be seen, we have to see.

My Cheese Drawer

All this talk of evil is getting to me. I'm going to clean something.

❧

Give me a bottle of glass cleaner and a paper towel. A broom. A duster. A toilet brush. I walk around my house sometimes and adjust picture frames on walls so they are all perfectly level and adjust the window blinds so that they all open along the same vertical line to each other. I straighten the rug and make sure the pillows are evenly placed on both sides of the couch.

This is a response to chaos and evil. I do not do it consciously. But I am aware that my house sparkles more as my soul sparkles less.

❧

Today, I am going to organize the cheese drawer in the fridge. Then I will send an email to my congressman.

❧

The war is taking up all the room in my brain. I remind myself to shower.

Rebuilding

Am levadad yishkon – the Bible states. We are a nation that dwells alone (Num. 23:9). Not always. But sometimes.

⁂

The director of a Hillel goes out for coffee with a colleague who has been posting violent pro-Palestine texts. She is unsure what to say so she says the truth.

"I feel so alone right now."

And the woman responds, "That must be so hard."

But what the director of the Hillel did not say is, "You make me feel so alone right now" because that is not what colleagues say to one another.

⁂

These weeks will be seared into my memory, into our collective consciousness: the shock, horror, disbelief, and anger will take years to process and will become the stuff of novels and movies, documentaries and museums. Broken hearts may be beyond repair, and then someone will place a broken heart gently into an exhibit for others to examine.

※

9/11 comes and goes during the war. It's been twenty-three years. A student mentions it in class and says, "None of us were even alive," then she looks at me because I was alive then. How can I explain what these very streets of New York looked like in the days and weeks after? All the nouns and adjectives in the world cannot describe the ash. Now other tall buildings soar to the same sky. A museum anchors the skyscrapers to the past. The broken hearts have been placed in an exhibit for others to examine.

※

I try to imagine the task of rebuilding a new world by standing beside Noah the moment he stepped out of the ark onto an apocalyptic terrain. He was so alone. So much responsibility rested on the slim shoulders of his righteousness. He offered a sacrifice first. A world destroyed by evil was restarted by an act of conscious giving.

※

I visit *Achim L'Chaim*, Brothers for Life, an Israeli nonprofit that pairs a newly injured soldier in Israel with a veteran of the military with the same injury for a lifetime of support. In that hospital bed, that soldier whose leg was blown off by an explosive wonders if anyone will date him, love him, hire him with his new "irregular" body. He does not want to work out at the gym or go to the local pool where well-meaning people stare at his sacrifice.

The soldier with a prosthetic limb or a gunshot wound to the stomach sees a future here for himself when he looks at someone else with the same injury who is thriving years later. He can work out and swim here where everyone has lost something and gained something. Friends for life.

❧

Maybe rebuilding is possible. For Jews, it is highly probable. It is what centuries or persecution has gifted us with: the capacity to make a new life anywhere.

❧

That soldier was once so alone. But now that soldier will never be alone. He will rebuild himself in humble company. "We must embrace the fragility that lends our lives beauty," writes the philosopher Todd May, "and at the same time withdraws that beauty from us. There is no straight path, nor a crooked one, that will lead us beyond all this."[20]

Exotic Mushrooms

I wear a white hairnet and sit for several hours packing shitake mushrooms in a small plant in Tekoa. The reservists who staff the plant are in the war now. The work must get done or the harvest is lost.

This is where the prophet Amos once served as a shepherd (Amos 1:1). It's a city that was fortified by King Rehoboam, Solomon's son (II Chron. 11:6),[21] and where King Jehoshaphat stopped nearby to pray (II Chron. 20:20). It was here that a "wise woman" convinced King David to allow his son Absalom to return (II Sam. 14:1–20).

In Tekoa there is a street called "Wise Woman." I'd like to live on a street with that name and think of that woman every time I turn the corner into that street.

❧

The exotic mushrooms must be sorted for size and quality and then placed on black Styrofoam beds to be covered in plastic and labeled. They should weigh 100 grams and then be sent on an assembly line to be wrapped. A university student supervises us for pay since there are no classes in the first months of the war. He tells us the weight does not need to be 100 grams exactly. "Go a little over, if you can't be exact." I like this message during war time. Give a little more rather than a little less.

☙

The two volunteers next to me are originally from Denmark. They travel together to volunteer. Yesterday it was tomatoes. Today it's mushrooms. Sometimes they are allowed to take home second-quality produce.

☙

I handle the mushrooms delicately to ensure that the caps and the tops stay together and that there are no nicks in their wondrous underside gills. The mushrooms weigh almost nothing. Each is oddly shaped. No two are alike. Their beauty lies in their deformity.

☙

For a minute I wonder if people will see the beauty of all those who are wounded because they are wounded.

There will be thousands now who live with the deformities of this war. And there are thousands who have already been living with the physical marks and scars of wars past.

No Excuses

Sometimes antisemites hate us because we are called the chosen people in the Hebrew Bible. I have spent my life trying to figure out what we've been chosen for. Responsibility? Suffering? Bringing our own stewardship and responsibility to a world crippled by pain?

I've heard scholars say we are not a chosen people but a choosing people. It is not a noun but a verb. Every faith, every family, and every child should be nurtured by the belief in their own specialness. It's what makes us strong and fills us with a sense of worthiness. But whatever it means, it is never a reason for the hate of others. It is an excuse.

I have learned the hard way never to make myself smaller to adjust to the size of the hate against me.

Terrorists don't want me to be small. They want me not to be.

Their goal is erasure.

I will not be erased.

"The price the Jews had to pay for being so loved so strongly by God has been being hated so strongly by humanity."[22]

I do not know if this is true, but it is difficult to regard our long-suffering as a sign of love.

⁂

Before there was a State of Israel, antisemites hated us for something else. For controlling banks. Or controlling the media. Or baking matza using the blood of Christian children. Or causing the Bubonic Plague. Or killing their god.

It does not take much to hate. It thrives in the absence of logic. Antisemitism loves the illogical. It lives for the conspiracy theory. It feeds on the insecurity of grown-up bullies who need to put Jews down to lift themselves up.

⁂

If I could, I would say to all the bullies of my childhood, "I am not the step ladder for your fragile ego. And don't pick anyone else either. Stop blaming me for your problems. I have enough of my own."

⁂

To antisemites, I am a Zionist pig or just a Zionist. The pig is assumed. And this is enough reason to hate me, and to beat my people with flag poles, or to kill and dismember them.

⁂

Stereotype threat is the internalization of a stereotype by the victim. It inhibits the freedom and growth of the victim. I must remind myself that I am not the worst thing that is said about me by those who do not know me.

"I imagine one of the reasons people cling to their hates so stubbornly is because they sense, once hate is gone, they will be forced to deal with pain," wrote James Baldwin to his fifteen-year-old nephew. He tried to teach his nephew how to be black in America, as if there were some way to map and negotiate irrational hatred. "A civilization is not destroyed by wicked people," Baldwin wrote. "It is not necessary that people be wicked but only that they be spineless."[23]

I wrestle with my spinelessness.

The cowardly lion in *The Wizard of Oz* confessed: "You're right. I am a coward. I haven't any courage at all." He had tears running down his fur when he said this, and his voice trembled.

Later, the lion met the Wizard, who taught the king of the jungle his first lesson: "You're a victim of disorganized thinking."

Baldwin confesses how narrow love can be. "When we were told to love *everybody*. I had thought that that meant everybody. But no. It applied only to those who believed as we did…and it did not apply to white people at all."[24]

Loving someone does not confer the right to hate someone else. Real love should be a love without borders.

Love Without Borders

The first chief rabbi of Palestine, Rabbi Abraham Isaac Kook (1865–1935), taught me about the porousness of love's borders:

> There is a person who sings the song of the Self. He finds everything, his complete spiritual satisfaction, within himself.
>
> And there is a person who sings the song of the Nation. He steps forward from his private self, which he finds narrow and insufficiently developed. He yearns for the heights. He clings with a sensitive love to the entirety of the Jewish nation and sings with it its song. He shares in its pains, is joyful in its hopes, speaks with exalted and pure thoughts regarding its past and its future, investigates its inner spiritual nature with love and a wise heart.
>
> There is a person whose soul is so broad that it expands beyond the border of Israel. It sings the song of humanity. This soul constantly grows broader with the exalted totality of humanity and its glorious image. He yearns for humanity's general enlightenment. He looks forward to its supernal perfection. From this source of life, he draws all of his thoughts and insights, his ideals and visions.

And there is a person who rises even higher until he unites with all existence, with all creatures, and with all worlds. And with all of them, he sings. This is the person who, engaged in the Chapter of Song every day, is assured that he is a child of the World-to-Come.

And there is a person who rises with all these songs together in one ensemble so that they all give forth their voices, they all sing their songs sweetly, each supplies its fellow with fullness and life: the voice of happiness and joy, the voice of rejoicing and tunefulness, the voice of merriment and the voice of holiness.

The song of the soul, the song of the nation, the song of humanity, and the song of the world mix together with this person at every moment and at all times.[25]

❧

It hurts when Jews sing the song of humanity but do not sing the song of their people.

It hurts when Jews sing the song of their people but do not sing the song of their humanity.

May there be a day soon when we can all sing every song without worrying about betrayal.

❧

A Jewish graduate student complains that his non-Jewish colleagues say nothing to him about October 7th. They are complicit in his eyes. He tells me that their silence is equivalent to kidnapping our babies.

I am shocked by the comparison. I listen because he is in pain. He vents and spews and makes wild comparisons and accusations. No one has compassion on our people, he barks.

Morning Has Broken

When his voice has softened, and I have acknowledged his indignation, I ask him quietly if he knows how many people died during the Armenian Genocide. Did he reach out and stand up for Black students after George Floyd was killed? Did he give money to humanitarian causes after the last major earthquake in Turkey?

He stares at me blankly. He sings the song of his people. He sings it loudly. But does he sing the song of humanity? Does he realize that there is a song?

What hurts more than pain is when someone else is silent in the face of suffering.

Growing into Consciousness

Life is not comfortable. We must be blunt and say it straight. Our job is not to make others comfortable. Our beautiful, precious young people must grow into consciousness and look ahead at the global responsibility that will one day lie upon them. It is not comfortable. We cannot hide who we are to make someone else comfortable.

Some young Jews may try to evade their birthright, but it will likely find them at this hour.

I hope they will hold their peers and colleagues and bosses accountable. Free speech is not free. It has consequences.

༄

Protestors put on masks so that they can spew hate and still get an internship in a white-shoe law firm. It doesn't work that way. It is illegal to protest in a mask. To the protestors I say, "Own your face."

The consequence of duplicitousness is to live without courage.

༄

I've heard the word "intersectionality" more times than I can count this past year, even though it's not a word I've heard often outside of campus life. I did not grow up with the word intersectionality in my dictionary. Kimberle Williams Crenshaw apparently coined it in 1989. Not too long ago. If you say the word intersectionality, most of America will look at you with bewilderment.

Intersectionality aims to unite those within the social categorizations of gender, race, class, to create interdependent groups to fight disadvantage and discrimination in society. Minorities who band together can protect the rights of each other, reduce the suffering of any individual group, and can smooth out impediments to success. On the face of it, Jews stand to benefit. Intersectionality would even seem an expression of our biblical mandate to care for the stranger and speak for the voiceless.

But when minority groups exclude some minorities – like Jews – it defeats its stated purpose. Critics of the theory claim its aims are ambiguous. It can be used as a tool of exclusion. It is frequently misunderstood and lacks uniform quantitative methods with which to interrogate its objectives. According to some critics, it is too subjective. We are under no obligation to embrace its dictates because it is intellectually fashionable.

෴

Sometimes Jews yearn for acceptance and sameness from the very people who care little for us.

෴

I waste so much time trying to get the approval of imaginary people.

෴

I wonder if indigenous people find it offensive when people introduce an event mentioning who once lived on the land where a particular event is taking place. One the one hand, it feels like an important acknowledgment of shame. On the other hand, it feels like a hollow token, like giving a child a cheap glittery toy that breaks instantly – as if mentioning who rightly has claim to this land, but will never have it, offers permission to proceed with business as usual. I don't know a solution for this. It's just what I feel when I hear these sentences from someone in a business suit standing with the authority of a podium.

༄

Statements that symbolically ritualize those who once lived somewhere are there to acknowledge the injustice and permit those to continue being who they have always been. The discomfort lasts a minute.

༄

This odd welcome mat of guilt – the recognition of people who once lived here but were robbed of their land – "advances a political thesis," argues Adam Kirsch, "that in a just world, every territory would be occupied only by the people who belong there."

Determining who belongs somewhere and who has the right to it now is complicated when the land has been lived in by two peoples for a long time, one dating to the Bible itself. Kirsch continues, "While anti-colonialism conceives of itself as a progressive, left-wing ideology, this understanding of the relationship between people and land is similar to that of fascism, which was also obsessed with the categories of native and alien."[26] This constant naming and shaming and division does not strike me as a way to relieve oppression but a way to reinforce it.

༄

Those who are pro-Hamas are quick to cite the settler-colonist narrative and compare Zionism to racism and Israel to apartheid. Such comparisons are easy. They require no mental work. Always be suspect of ease. It risks intellectually laziness. Cornell Law School's Legal Information Institute defines settler colonialism as "a system of oppression based on genocide and colonialism that aims to displace a population of a nation and replace it with a new settler population."[27] America, of course, becomes the biggest offender in this definition. Does anyone believe America will decolonize?

Maybe it would be a better use of time to work on societal problems that can create genuine change.

※

We can continue going back in time to identify the very first humans to settle in any particular place. I wonder when the clock starts and how we would determine it. The clock does not start, however, in 1948.

※

The European Union finally condemned Hamas for using innocent civilians, especially Gazan children, as human shields. It took thirty-seven days of this happening for a statement, then it was back to a steady stream of attacks on Israel. I await a protest against Hamas' use of children as shields in Gaza.

※

Who cannot cry over the loss of Palestinian life? The test of a human being is the capacity to cry over the lives of people on the other side of a war. We drop small seeds of grape juice on white plates at the Passover Seder to remember that Egyptians died when we were saved. Grape juice will not save them but remembering them softens our hard-heartedness.

※

Who is crying for us now but ourselves?

Different Worlds

I get two newspapers. Read two different newspapers, and two different worlds reveal themselves that are actually the same world.

~

In one newspaper, a hospital in Gaza has been bombed by Israeli occupiers fighting against militants.

In one newspaper, the tunnels under a hospital in Gaza are being used as a terrorist command center stockpiled with weapons.

~

The truth is verified. But the newspaper does not apologize or issue a retraction. It offers an editor's note.

~

In another newspaper, 290,000 people marched on the National Mall for Israel. In another newspaper, it was tens of thousands until this morning, when it was downgraded to just thousands. I was there. You can deceive me with false information when I was not there to see it with my own eyes. You cannot pretend I am blind. But if I am fact-checking, I must also admit that I did not personally count all of the people.

⁂

Numbers are the great casualty of war besides its actual casualties.[28] The result of a war shaped by social media is that I trust nothing and no one. I am increasingly suspicious of motives and the press. World leaders are no longer authority figures for me. Their numbers are meaningless. Without trust, I've become more solitary. I do not believe the words of people who occupy positions I once revered. The person on the screen says, I see you. He insists. But he does not see me.

It is hard to live in a world without trust.

⁂

"Kindly do not attempt to cloud the issues with facts," warned Mr. Banks in *Mary Poppins*.

⁂

All of the literary magazines and periodicals I get in the mail ignore this war. That tall, distinct paper periodical. That weekly magazine with cartoons. There are still feature pieces, restaurant reviews, lists of new goings-on, but the fire on the other side of the world is met with silence.

I see myself nowhere on these pages.

Dominant and Subordinate

"The dominant group is seen as the norm for humanity," writes Beverly Tatum in *Why Are All the Black Kids Sitting Together in the Cafeteria?* "Dominant groups," she observes, "do not like to be reminded of the existence of inequality."[29] Rationalizations are created so that the dominant groups can live comfortably among those who are subordinates. Some groups, she writes, "can be dominant in one setting and subordinate in other ways."[30]

Jews in university: dominant/subordinate.

❧

Jews have always been the subordinates to someone else's dominance but overrepresented on college campuses as students, faculty, and administrators. The world of ideas, knowledge, research, and scholarship has been a second home.

Higher education first took the form of the *beit midrash* – the study hall. Today, study halls are still full in virtually every country where Jews have ever lived in considerable number. There are more *yeshivot* than in any other period of Jewish history.

Morning Has Broken

As far back as the sixth century, Jews attended the University of Jundishapur in Sassanid Persia. They studied in the Bayt al-Kikma, the House of Wisdom, in Baghdad in the ninth century. A Jew attended medical school in the fourteenth century at the University of Montpellier. In the fifteenth and sixteenth centuries, Jewish names were included among the students and faculty of European universities, especially those in Italy.

One Jew, the Hebrew grammarian Elijah Levita, was invited to be a professor at the University of Paris in the fifteenth century. He refused because other Jews were not permitted to live in Paris at the time. He chose not to separate himself physically from his people even when others separated him intellectually.

※

University College London was founded by the philosopher Jeremy Bentham, among others, because Jews and other minorities were denied entrance to Cambridge and Oxford.

In Nazi Germany, Jews were forbidden to study certain subjects in university or at certain universities or get promoted as faculty.

In the Former Soviet Union, Jews who declared their desire to go to Israel often lost their places in university.

Jews in universities in the United States once faced quotas and outward discrimination.

Jewish students – you, my dear friends – thought that in the twenty-first century, the campus was yours for the taking. Now you feel less secure. The death of that privilege must be grieved. It is an immense loss.

※

I try not to internalize today's vulgar disrespect. I try not to wonder if maybe there is a problem with me if so many people who share lives similar to mine make me feel rejected, vulnerable, and powerless.

I may be subordinate, a minority among minorities, but I do not deserve to be treated as a subordinate when I still feel so much love for the world.

A Mother's Love

A mother's love is not insignificant in times of war. It is the love of a woman waiting for a son to return from battle. Sisera's mother in the book of Judges waited by the window for a son to return who would never return. And although Sisera was an enemy, the Bible pauses for a moment so that we stand by that window with this woman in her anguish, this woman who has no name other than the designation of someone's mother.

There is an affection that a woman – that any person with children – can feel for an enemy's child simply because of the shared bond of parenthood. It's in Rachel Goldberg's plea for her kidnapped son Hersh: "Every single person in Gaza has a mother, or had a mother at some point. And I would say this, then, as mother to other mothers: If you see Hersh, please help him. I think about it a lot. I really think I would help your son, if he was in front of me, injured, near me."[31]

There is a fierceness to a mother's outrage that babies are held in captivity while too many are silent. They wait by the window.

Basic Training

The soldier wears a uniform. The soldier has undergone basic training. The soldier is, more or less, prepared.

※

The Jewish student in the Diaspora wears no uniform and has undergone no basic training for this. The Jewish student is not likely prepared.

Uncomplicated Love

It's a complicated time for some to love Israel. But, for me, right now, it has become a blessedly uncomplicated time to love Israel.

※

I am tired of complicated love. Sometimes love is not complicated at all. Life is exhausting if every meaningful relationship we have is complicated.

※

I try not to underestimate the force and goodness of simple love.

※

Sometimes I make the mistake of thinking that unity and solidarity requires the totality of my commitment. Either I am one with my people or I am not. Unity does not mean agreement with everyone about everything, I tell myself, but does that include those I intensely disagree with? Lately, I have been kinder to myself. When I do not feel total unity, I reserve those pieces of myself that fit nowhere for a special box labeled composite emotions.

༄

It is always the enemy who reminds me we are one. I am a member of a nomadic tribe even if it stays in one location for a few hundred years. In this tribe, if I don't know you, chances are high that I know someone who knows you. But even if I don't, our bonds are psychic.

You are part of my extended family, and it is my duty to invest in and protect this small human family. Jews who have been at home in the world can also feel rejected by that world, and it is in these times of exposure and danger that we need our people. And we need uncomplicated love.

That is what I tell myself when I see photos of thousands of Israeli protestors spilling out of Hostage Square on a Saturday night.

༄

People play Jewish geography to map out their own situatedness in proximity to someone only a degree of separation away. It reduces Judaism to who you know now. And then the game fans out to all those connected to the past.

Every invisible line of connection is suddenly made visible.

The Gift of Particularism

Although we are members of a tribe, but we cannot behave tribally. We must speak the universal from our particularism.

※

In his acceptance speech for the Nobel Prize in literature, Isaac Bashevis Singer acknowledged that the very particular conditions where Yiddish thrived were noted by the Swedish Academy: "In spite of all the disenchantments and all my skepticism, I believe that the nations can learn much from those Jews, their way of thinking, their way of bringing up children, their finding happiness where others see nothing but misery and humiliation."

The ghetto raised Jews with a way of thinking that "does not demand and command, but it muddles through, sneaks by, smuggles itself amidst the powers of destruction, knowing somewhere that God's plan for Creation is still at the very beginning."[32]

Singer's universal themes took their color from their particularism. Love of the world originates in love of the self.

※

Jews have generally held the banner high for humanitarianism. Humanitarianism is not distinct from Judaism but an outgrowth of it. It is the voice of the ancient prophet echoing into the future soul of every Jew to watch and work the garden that is this earth.

⁂

If the prophet's voice echoes in us, it is God's voice that echoes through the prophet, placing the bar of our responsibility to those in need or in danger impossibly high.

"I, the Lord, in My grace, have summoned you, and I have grasped you by the hand. I created you, and appointed you a covenant people, a light of nations, opening eyes deprived of light, rescuing prisoners from confinement, from the dungeon those who sit in darkness" (Is. 42:6–7).

God holds my hand and walks with me in the valley of the shadow of death and says, "Look around. Have mercy. Do something. Go to the darkness. Bring others to the light. Stare at confinement and imagine freedom."

⁂

Sometimes it's not mercy that moves me but indignation. Injustice fills me with torment and turmoil. Something must be done. The world is burning, and someone must run into the fire. But if I run into the fire, will someone save me?

⁂

Rabbi A. J. Heschel wrote that the prophet saw and heard what others refused to see and hear. The Hebrew prophet feels fiercely. "The prophet's word is a scream in the night. While the world is at ease and asleep, the prophet feels the blast from heaven."[33]

Rethinking Social Justice

Without knowing someone's pain we can never understand their anger.

❦

I worry that a casualty of this war will be social justice. On difficult days, I care less about a world Isaiah told us to care a great deal about. I am ashamed of my indifference.

❦

Social justice flourishes when it's a mixture of compassion and outrage. This is the basis of *tikkun olam*, a value axiomatic to Judaism. Many were nursed on the milk of *tikkun olam* as the chief expression of their Judaism. Individually and together, we will change the world.

❦

The translation of "*tikkun*" influences our faith in the world as it currently is. If it is broken in places, we will *repair* it. If it is in fragments, we will *fix* it. If it is good, we will *improve* it. If it is improved, we will *perfect* it. One two-syllable word. A myriad of meanings. All point heavenward.

❧

The expression *tikkun olam* appears first in the Mishna, collected rabbinic sayings from the earliest centuries of the common era. It appears in the closing of our prayers, in *Aleinu*, in the second paragraph, where we seek *"to perfect the world in the kingdom of God."* We believe that we perfect the world in partnership with God. God is always in the equation.

The idea then developed into a central concept of sixteenth-century Lurianic kabbala. The world is a broken vessel. It shattered into millions of pieces. Our human task is to find the spark of godliness in each fragment and put the pieces together again to heal the world. Each good act we do affects the very cosmos.

❧

If Jewish mysticism seems too esoteric, Arik Einstein, the popular Israeli singer, offered a theme song for this generation:

> *Ani va'ata nishane et ha'olam.*
> *You and I, we'll change the world.*
> *You and I, then all will follow.*
> *Others have said it before me.*
> *But it doesn't matter.*
> *You and I, we'll change the world.*
>
> *You and I, we'll try from the beginning.*
> *It will be tough for us, no matter. It's not too bad.*
> *Others have said it before me.*
> *But it doesn't matter.*
> *You and I, we'll change the world.*

❧

There is this world, and then there is the more enlightened, brighter world that we can create together – you and me. It is within our reach if we dream and aspire enough. Our humanity is constantly evolving and advancing spiritually so that we become more loving and inclusive with every new generation. I have held tightly to this naïve worldview even when it is threatened by a gruesome reality. Some days, it feels like I am holding a little sign with a hackneyed inspirational saying to mask my true anxieties.

※

At 1:58 this morning, all our smoke alarms went off. I jumped out of bed and ran through the house, blinking in the light, trying to figure out what happened. I thought someone had broken into our house and set it on fire. Jew-haters. They must be all over the neighborhood wreaking havoc.

I could not let go of that fear even after we turned the alarms off, one by one. Me. Who used to leave the door unlocked all day.

It's nothing, I tell myself. But across the world, there are sirens, and they are not nothing.

My anxieties are unmasked. I am tired all day.

※

The work of the world is not on a bumper sticker. It's in the covenantal commitments we make in the name of service. We have stood beside others to seek justice because we are obligated in Jewish law and because we are obligated by virtue of our humanity. Jews are ethically obligated to care about the moral and spiritual welfare of society at large. Rabbi Joseph Soloveitchik wrote, "We stand shoulder to shoulder with the rest of civilized society over against an order which defies us all."[34]

We stand with others to defy moral chaos because this is our world, the only one we will ever have.

※

We perfect the world because no matter how good it is, it can always be better. And no matter how bad it is, it will always be worth saving.

⁂

In Deuteronomy, there's a puzzling contradiction. First, we are told, "There shall be no needy among you – since the Lord your God will bless you in the land that the Lord your God is giving you as a hereditary portion" (Deut. 15:4). If we live virtuously, poverty will be eliminated entirely. Then, three verses later, poverty is back: "If, however, there is a needy person among you … do not harden your heart and shut your hand against your needy kinsman" (Deut. 15:7). The first verse describes the economically fair and equitable society we are tasked to create. The second assures us this ideal is unlikely.

In this contradiction lies the revolution that is Judaism. Into the ancient world we were given a guiding portrait of a perfect society. The aspiration appears first. Then, quickly, after reality and poverty abounds, our duties to society set in. We cannot and should not accept a world that is anything short of a just society. Anything less is a moral failure on our part. There should not be a poor person living amongst us if we share what we have with all who are in need.

God gave us the vision and asked us to be stakeholders in the ongoing creation of righteous communities.

⁂

The Talmud depicts an exchange between God and each of us when our time on this earth is over. God will ask us a series of questions to measure the worth of our lives.

Did you deal honestly in business?

Did you study?

Did you have children – demonstrating your commitment to an unseen future?

I fear that day. The hardest question God will ask me is, "Did you hope for the world's redemption?"[35] It's best for me to answer the questions now. Later might be too late.

⁂

Leaving the world a better place is the work of a lifetime and the measure of a life. Jewish law mandates that we protect the oppressed, the penniless, the homeless, and the downtrodden. *"Learn to do good; seek justice, relieve the oppressed, judge the fatherless, plead for the widow"* (Is. 1:17). Isaiah tells us that goodness must be learned. It is not always obvious.

"Let my people go." Let all people go. We were told dozens of times in the Bible to protect the stranger and give voice to the voiceless because we were once strangers, and we were once voiceless.

⁂

If we have stood with you, please stand with us. At the very least, do not stand against us.

The Validation of Outsiders

"Israel was not created in order to disappear – Israel will endure and flourish," said President John F. Kennedy. "It is the child of hope and the home of the brave. It can neither be broken by adversity nor demoralized by success. It carries the shield of democracy, and it honors the sword of freedom."[36]

⁂

Kennedy warms me until I ask myself why I am so desperate for crumbs of praise from outsiders.

A Better World

Rabbi Sacks wrote, "Peace involves a profound crisis of identity. The boundaries of self and other, friend and foe, must be redrawn."[37] This is also true of hate. It redraws boundaries and closes certain people out while intensifying belonging for others.

✌

We changed the clocks, but the situation is still the same.

We changed the clocks, but there is still time to change.

✌

The day the war broke out, we began reading the Book of Genesis anew. The first eleven and a half chapters are about the creation of the world and the first human beings. The end of chapter 11 through chapter 25 contains the stories of Abraham and his family. The rest, until chapter 50, are the stories of Jacob and his family.

We do not begin Genesis with the story of the Jews but with the human family. Only later do we taper the focus to Abraham and his small, nascent family.

I was born – all of us were born – with a universal mission, to find companionship among animals, to steward a garden, and to create sacred communities. On this past Simchat Torah, as the war in Israel was beginning, in the Diaspora, we were repeating the Genesis story that is our narrative beginning.

❧

When my faith totters, I tell myself I was born into a world far greater than myself.

The First Protestor

Abraham, the first Jew, was a protestor. To be a protester is a badge of courage. It means that by debating God, you are in a dialogic relationship with God. God expects a good argument.

Abraham called out God's plan to destroy Sodom. Those innocent and righteous people within the immoral city's walls deserved saving. If there weren't fifty, there were forty. If there weren't twenty, there were ten. "Far be it from You to do such a thing, to bring death upon the innocent as well as the guilty, so that innocent and guilty fare alike. Far be it from You! Shall not the Judge of all the earth deal justly?" (Gen. 18:25).

The citizens of Sodom did not espouse Abraham's newly discovered monotheism or share his friendship with God. This was all the more reason to challenge God. You cannot build a nation on injustice. Your God, too, must be righteous.

※

In his *Letters to a Young Activist*, Todd Gitlin describes the threat of nuclear war in the 1960s that drove him to knock on doors, distribute pamphlets, campaign for political candidates, and challenge the prevailing norms that birthed the threat. Now we have a new word for those who engage in these behaviors: activists. Then, he and his friends didn't use this word. His parents' generation called them protestors: "Outsiders called us *protestors* – but protest was only one of our faces. We were trying to build – to be – a better society."[38]

I do not want to defend my right to exist. I have every right exist. Instead, I want to protest against those who tell me I must defend my existence.

Choosing Life

The Torah teaches emphatically, *"uvacharta bachayim"* (Deut. 30:19) because sometimes, in our long and difficult history, death has been a choice. Giving in to despair has its own seductions. The Torah combats this resignation and abdication of the self with two resounding words: choose life.

❧

We do not choose life once. We choose it by the minute again and again, as a soulful friend reminded me just six days after October 7th: "…we will fight for our world of love and life and growth and kindness with a ferocity that our enemies' fight for death simply cannot match. And we will go on forever choosing life."[39]

This is why Jews wear necklaces with a *chai* (life), toast each other with *l'chaim* (to life), or write checks to charity or bat mitzva girls in multiples of eighteen (the numerical equivalent of life).

❧

I saw a photograph yesterday morning of an Israeli soldier in uniform on a break with his family. He was sitting and feeding his baby with a bottle. Prepared to die, he was affirming life.

※

One day, on a family vacation to Italy, I stood on the grounds outside the Colosseum. While the tourists took photos, I turned away and wept. This place represented the dominance of Rome over Jews long ago. Then we were powerless and prevented from expressing our faith.

But as I came back to my family and we walked the street, a man dressed in a red gladiator outfit, who charged a Euro to take a photo, saw my husband's yarmulka. In Hebrew, he said *"Ma nishma?"* – How are you? Imagine that. An Israeli dressed as a gladiator to make a few euros.

Suddenly, the narrative changed. I felt immense relief. The Colosseum stands as a ruin. The language once spoken inside it is dead. The gladiator spectacles are long past.

We were ancient, and now we are modern. We had a language then, and we have that language again.

Rebirth is stranger than birth and maybe more powerful. This is why we must choose life even at the cost of death.

The Mountain Man

In the book of Exodus, only two chapters after the Israelites crossed the sea into safety, they encountered the most immoral enemy they ever faced: the Amalekites, the Hamas of their day. One day, when they least suspected it, this killing force appeared.

The Amalekites attacked the defenseless – the women, the children, the elderly – from behind. There was little time for the Israelites to celebrate their freedom. Moses sent Joshua to find men to fight the war with him while Moses went up on a hill with his nephew Hur, a young military leader, and his brother Aaron, a High Priest. Moses brought his staff and held it up for all to see: "Whenever Moses held up his hand, Israel prevailed; but whenever he let down his hand, Amalek prevailed" (Ex. 17:11).

It was the same staff used to part the waters and execute the miracles that bought the people their liberty. Once, it even turned into a snake and back in Moses' hand. The entire time Moses held the staff up in the war against the Amalekites, the Israelites were successful. If his arms failed, his people failed. Aaron and Hur sat him on a rock and helped him hold up that staff.

Leaders hold up their people during wartime.

Moses did not hold up a sword, a more obvious choice in war. He gave that task to Joshua. Moses held up the most basic tool of a shepherd, reminding the people of their values and his. We are a flock. God is our shepherd and savior. Moses, too, was a shepherd and savior.

※

Moses was a mountain man. When we first meet him shepherding his flock, he was heading to Mount Horev. When he received the Ten Commandments, he climbed up Mount Sinai and appeared there again to seek God's atonement after the golden calf debacle. Right before he died, Moses scaled Mount Nevo and enjoyed a striking aerial view of the land he would never enter.

Yet after the first Amalekite attack, Moses, staff in hand, goes up on a hill – a *giva* – not a mountain. At war, leaders need to see and be seen.

Leaders cannot be remote from those they serve at times of crisis. The people have to see their leader fight just as hard or harder than they are fighting. Each person in this story brings a specific, singular talent that is theirs alone in battle. Moses and his staff represented redemptive hope in the triumph of the weak. His staff worked miracles. He was a walking miracle.

※

"In Israel," David Ben-Gurion once said, "in order to be a realist, you must believe in miracles."

※

In this war, everyone is on the frontlines of something. Some are on the actual frontlines. Some are home taking care of everything else. Some live far away and send donations to the charities that feed and outfit those on the frontlines. Some provide online therapy. Some babysit. Some write. Some pray.

❧

Moses took his staff, not the sword, as his symbol of resistance. His people were a flock, not an army. He moved in the world as a guide and protector, not a soldier. His strength came from influence, not power.

❧

Wars are fought in the field and in the soul. Moses was an advocate held up by a solider and a priest. Who held up Hur and Aaron?

❧

In wars, people are left at home to be the caregivers. Caregivers also need caring. During war, wives, husbands, children, mothers, and fathers need to be held up.

❧

Winning a war requires advocacy, military strategy, and deep faith. Soldiers fight on the battlefield. Advocates speak truth to power. These roles require training, experience, and access.

Faith is the currency of every soul. When Moses held up his staff, "his hands remained steady until the sun set" (Ex. 17:12). The Hebrew word for steady here is *emuna*. This is the same word for faith. Moses held his hands up with the faith that one day he could put his hands down.

❧

Those who are religious pray, recite psalms, and study harder so that this war ends and Israel wins. They gather, sing, and make meaning. This is religious activism. It inspires unity and comfort and affirms goodness and kindness. But sometimes religious activists forget that to win a war you must also write letters to politicians and newspapers, lobby, rally, vote, and protest.

༄

There are those who advocate, write letters, lobby, rally, vote, and protest. This is political activism. It is often uncomfortable and involves confrontation and outrage against injustice. But sometimes political activists forget that to win a war you must also gather, pray, and sing because it stirs the soul, creates community, and diminishes isolation.

༄

Students ask, "Will going to a rally make any difference? So many other people will be there." People must think simultaneously that they can move the world and that they can do nothing to move the world. The first thought helps us show up. The second thought prevents haughtiness.

༄

When the war against the Amalekites was over, God told Moses to write it all down: "Inscribe all this as a reminder…" (Ex. 17:14). In the Exodus story, nowhere is it recorded that after all the miracles in Egypt and God's mighty deliverance, Moses had to write it all down. After *this* sudden attack by a vicious enemy, Moses was told to write it all down.

When there is peace and quiet, we might forget that genuine evil exists and persists. We let down our armor because we crave a belief in the world's enduring worth. In the same verse, Moses was told to read what he had written aloud to Joshua: "I will utterly blot out the memory of Amalek from under heaven!"

Never forget. Expect sudden violence. Name evil. Write it all down. When antisemitism quiets, we risk not believing it is possible. We let down our guard. We forget that evil persists. Jewish history is a series of ceasefires.

Blue and White

The fighting and even the first ceasefire brought a thick solidarity to Israel and its friends. The tribe has gotten stronger. The flags are out on streets, cars, highways, stores, balconies. I've never seen more Israeli flags.

❧

Rabbi Soloveitchik, in his essay "The Symbolism of Blue and White," discusses the significance of each color in relation to *tzitzit*, the ritual fringes. "Symbolically," the Rav writes, "the color white denotes clarity, distinctness, rationality, that which is self-evident." White also signifies purity.

❧

In *tzitzit*, there are several threads of white woven with only one thread of majestic blue, *tekhelet*. Blue is the color of the heavens, directing our eyes upward. The color "focuses our thoughts on the grand mysteries of human experience which elude our precise understanding. The seas and heavens are boundless and beyond human reach."[40]

This joining of colors – white and blue – is symbolic of the dichotomies of human existence: the stable and the fragile, the transparent and the mysterious.

Rabbi Soloveitchik then turns from the white and blue to their meaning as complements to each other.

> The same dichotomy between being on *terra firma* and on shifting sand is also experienced in our personal lives. We have all had periods, even of an extended nature, which are rational, planned, and predictable, when we feel that we have a hold on events. At other times, however, mystery and puzzlement intervene, dislocating the pattern of our lives and frustrating all our planning. No one can say, "The world and I have always gotten together reasonably, happily, and successfully, with ambitions always being realized. I have never been defeated." Stark and harsh reality often imposes the bizarre and the irrational, leaving us stupefied, shocked, and bereft. Inexplicable events render us humbled. This is the *tekhelet* of human experience.[41]

The Rav's conclusion offers us a new way to look at the Israeli flag. Its durability and meaning are an evocative symbol of hope: "Only a people sustained by *tekhelet* could be motivated to reconstitute a state after two thousand years of exile...We are sustained by *tekhelet*, even when it is only a vision and temporarily obscured. The garment of Jewish life will yet possess both blue and white, and our historical yearnings and sacrifices will be vindicated."[42]

And may it be so. And may it be so.

*

In August of the war, we walk to shul one Friday night and come home to a fright. The American and Israeli flags have been cut off from our flagpole and are gone. Someone must have known the exact hour we attend synagogue. There are several lawn signs in our neighborhood that say "Hamas abducted our family. Bring them home." Those are easy pickings, yet every sign remained in place.

*

Near our flagpole is a swing we roped high onto a tree branch that everyone in the neighborhood uses. No one need ask permission. It is next to a bench so that those who are not on the swing can sit comfortably. The bench says, "Love Your Neighbor."

※

On Shabbat morning, I went outside to pick up my newspapers and saw my immediate neighbors, a lovely non-Jewish couple, walking by and told them about our flags. They were shocked and upset. "Can we let everyone know?" one asked.

"Yes, please let everyone know."

The Pause

The first ceasefire brought no relief. It was just a waiting game until rules were once again broken, giving time to re-arm and re-group and re-visit the horrors of war.

❧

It's early morning, and I haven't finished my coffee. My husband sits on the couch next to me, looks straight into my eyes, and says, "The ceasefire is over. I didn't want to tell you while you were in bed."

We say nothing else. There is nothing to say. We know what this means.

❧

We are all members of more than one tribe. Tribes within tribes. Rings and rings of overlapping and sometimes contradictory identities. The tribe of humanity should spread its cloak on us all. But until it does, I will stay within the smaller ring of trust that now feels like the only ring.

Symbology

In battle, we need symbols. We are not only held up by our military strength. We are held up by our values and our faith.

❧

Soldiers everywhere are suddenly wearing tzitzit. People throughout Israel and the Diaspora are tying these strings and knots. It's an ancient spiritual defense that reminds the person who wears it of God: "You will remember all the commandments of God to perform them, and you shall not wander after your hearts and after your eyes" (Num. 15:39).

Stay true to your mission. Let the fringes speak.

❧

There are other Jewish symbols on the battlefield now. People who are not observant want *mezuzot* that contain the mission statement of the Jewish people and have the Hebrew letter *"shin"* on the outside that stands for *Shada-i*, God as Protector.

Special chapters of Talmud are printed and sent to soldiers so they can keep up their daily study of each folio page. Soldiers carry army-green portable arks holding small Torah scrolls to be read from on Mondays, Thursdays, and *Shabbatot*. The Torah, as it did in the book of Numbers, accompanies us into war.

All of these symbols may outlast the war if they are not just tokens of desperation.

Moses eventually put the staff down as normal domestic life returned. The way you know life returned to normal is that the Israelites complained about the food and water.

Complaining is a luxury.

Say a Little Prayer

Praying helps me. It's a way of speaking. Sometimes it's easy to pray; sometimes it's hard. There is so much to pray for that I hope the feeling attaches itself to the words and that the words fly up. *"Sustainer of the living with kindness. Resurrector of the dead with great mercy. Supporter of the fallen. Healer of the sick. Releaser of the imprisoned. Fulfiller of His faithfulness to those who sleep in the dust."*

Hear me, God. End this war. Lift the fallen. Release the imprisoned. Please. Pretty please.

❧

Today will be a better day. A non-Jewish friend called and left a message. "Tell me what you're praying for so I can pray for the same thing." I am nourished by that message for the next several hours.

❧

Do not forget the kindnesses, I remind myself, that war brings off the battlefield.

Before Shabbat in Israel, I enter a flower shop and buy a gift. The shopkeeper hands me back my credit card and says, "We should hear good news soon." I say, "Amen."

⁂

I wake up, go to the kitchen, and check my phone but then remind myself to pray and study first so that my day is not reactive. Then I remind myself that when I check the news it gives me more reason to pray.

⁂

It is *Tachanun*, the post-*Amida* prayer, that affects me the most. In synagogue, I put my head down on my left arm as part of the choreography of the humble petitioner an;d reflect on my existential insignificance. This is easy for me.

> *Guardian of Israel, guard the remnant of Israel, and let not Israel perish, who say, "Hear Israel."*
>
> *Guardian of the unique nation, guard the remnant of the unique people, and let not the unique nation perish, who proclaim the Oneness of Your Name: Adon-ai is our God, Adon-ai is One.*
>
> *Guardian of the holy nation, guard the remnant of the holy people and let not the holy nation perish who repeat the threefold sanctification to the Holy One.*
>
> *Your people are held in contempt by all who surround us. And now, listen our God, to the prayers of Your servant and to supplications; and let Your radiant countenance shine upon Your desolate Sanctuary for Your sake, my Master.*

Your desolate sanctuary is the Temple that is no more. It is also the empty Israeli street today that is usually filled with tourists. Some restaurants haven't opened in weeks. The airport was desolate. You could hear an echo in the hall at Ben Gurion that usually looks and sounds like a Middle Eastern bazaar. The marble floor shined. I never noticed the floors before.

Protest Jewelry

Someone in Israel gave me a dog tag. In Hebrew it says, "Our heart remains in Gaza." In English it says, "Bring them home now!" I will wear it until the last of them come home.

Wearing jewelry is not advocacy, but it keeps the hostages literally near my heart lest an hour or day go by without thinking about them. Babies and college students. Grandfathers and teenagers.

I put the day of the war on the tag each morning with medical tape and marker.

⋆

On Friday night, I light an extra set of Shabbat candles for a hostage in Gaza who cannot light Shabbat candles. The rest that they portend is no rest for someone in a tunnel.

⋆

The day I took off the Anatoly Sharansky bracelet I wore throughout high school and college, I also took the poster of his face off my bedroom wall. He was liberated. It was glorious.

Morning Has Broken

We marched and protested. I went to New York and Washington, DC and Jerusalem marching for Soviet Jewry and then to the Soviet Union during my last year of college. Then the Iron Curtain opened. And I thought to myself, there is nothing our people can't do.

But today, I feel defeated by this war. There is nothing we can do. We can't bring any of the dead back.

I gave a talk, and a woman rushed home to fetch her metal bracelet from the Soviet Jewry movement; she proudly showed it to me. It was the Jewish protestor's Crown Jewel. The small metal cuff brings back a flood of memories.

Where is my protest bracelet? I must have thrown it out all those years ago. The work was done. He was home.

But it's not like me to throw something like that away. It represented too many years of my life.

※

Some months after Natan Sharansky walked across the Glienicke Bridge to his liberation; he came to Yeshiva University. I was a college student and watched him carried aloft on the shoulders of students while a room of over a thousand sang songs to celebrate his freedom. It filled me with enough hope to devote my life to the Jewish people.

There is an endorphin surge of optimism when the work we do together finally pays off. The work changes us. It changed me.

※

I dreamed about the day when Hersh Goldberg-Polin would come into that same auditorium. Everyone would fill the room with song and good cheer and revel in the miracle. We would thank God for this day and bless it. Over a thousand young people would conclude that when you work hard and work together, there is nothing you cannot achieve. Their hearts would be full, and some would see that day as a decisive crossroads in their own faith and leadership.

But that day will never come.

Our Fault

Maybe it is our fault, the fault of my generation. We tell our children constantly how special they are. Remember that *New Yorker* cartoon? The kid holds a trophy bigger than himself and says to his father, "Look, Dad, we lost."

We told our children that everyone's a winner. We did not prepare our children for the hurt of the world. We did not have good things to say about leaders and global problems. And now that world hasn't stopped disappointing them. It has disappointed me, too, but I was reared for disappointment.

❧

When I grew up, I was made to feel small. I am short. This came naturally to me. The teacher was always right. The adults never said sorry. Leadership was noble. The world was an extraordinary place, damaged, to be sure, but remarkable, nevertheless. We were advised to serve and, if we were lucky, we would be worthy of the world's grace.

❧

But I picked up my children when they fell. I worried when they competed. I saw their Bs turn into B pluses and sometimes even into As. I heard other parents claim that the teachers are wrong. The adults should apologize. In college, teachers issued trigger warnings so students could excuse themselves from pain before it even arrived.

I'm sorry.

✢

Maybe this war has changed something in our children and in all of us. Maybe the peace and relative quiet Jews enjoyed in American was really a historical aberration.

We will be more prepared for pain now.

✢

It's day #283 of the war. Israel's Supreme Court has extended the time of army service from two years and eight months to three years. End of reservist duty moved from age forty to forty-five and officers from age forty-five to fifty. Much is being asked of so many, and still it is not enough. It makes those of us in the Diaspora contemplate the sacrifices we are prepared to make. The extension of time spotlights those in Israel who do not send their children off to war but still expect the army's protection. This will cause more internal strife.

But, then again, I didn't serve in the American army, nor did my children. I count on the American army for protection. Maybe it's different when there's a mandatory draft, and when you're a small country with no friendly neighbors. I don't know.

✢

A friend from Israel calls. Her sons and son-in-law are either going in to serve or coming back or going in again. She is infuriated by the prolonged refusal of some to fight at all. "They don't even pray for our soldiers," she says indignantly. "I used to tolerate it because I believe in the importance of Torah study. But now I'm angry." Her boys serve. They don't have a choice. But if they did have a choice, serving would be their choice. They also study. It's not easy. They have to find the time on a navy ship or beside an armored vehicle, maybe very early in the morning or very late at night. The Talmud volumes they carry are pocket-sized, created for troops so that they can honor the totality of their commitments wherever they are.

❧

The new rule extending army service is only four months of additional time, but a lot can happen in four months. A young person can start university or travel the world. Or lie on a couch and recuperate. Someone can fall in love in four months.

❧

I imagine a soldier in Gaza counting down the days until he can sit down with his family and eat a home-cooked meal lovingly prepared when he hear the news. He must stay in Gaza longer. He has at least 120 more days of hell to go.

❧

They will be lions, this new generation. But even lions need a rest.

The Long, Long Road

All over the streets there are signs in Hebrew that say, "The victorious nation is not afraid of the long road." This implies that the road will be long, and we should not be afraid. But I am afraid. And it's monotonous being on the same road for so long.

※

The third-century Talmud sage Rabbi Tarfon articulated the complex nexus between obligation and complacency when he advised his disciples to find a balance: "It is not your duty to finish the work, but neither are you at liberty to neglect it."[43]

When we work for a cause, we hope we will live to see our work complete. But we also recognize that no matter how hard we try to bring awareness to homelessness, malaria in Africa, climate change, domestic abuse, animal rights, or any other cause, ignorance, cruelty, and exploitation will exist as long as humans exist.

The road is long. But we are on it. We must do our share and then pass it on to others to do theirs. If we do not do this work, we will not be able to pass it on.

The dark side of human nature continues to surprise and befuddle us. It also keeps us employed.

※

Fighting for justice and peace and wholeness can be a full-time job without retirement benefits. Yet according to Rabbi Tarfon, it's a part-time job with benefits. But there is also no retirement.

※

Pete Davis, a writer and social activist, worries that there are too many big causes in the world and too few people devoted to tackling them seriously. He is looking for what he calls "long-haul heroes." He's had enough of superficial commitments. He advises young people not to become fully subsumed in causes but to enter into "faithful relationships" with them. "It's not about ironing out all uncertainty but about being willing to temper our doubts enough to have commitments that last a little bit longer, are a little bit stickier, and have a little bit more authority over us."[44]

※

Find a cause to die for and live for it. Rabbi Tarfon does not ask us to complete the work. He asks that we be long-haul heroes and stay on the road.

※

It is day #346 of the war. The road just got longer. I am unsure where it leads. God, give me a traveler's prayer for this long road.

In Righteousness and Justice

"*I will betroth you to me forever; I will betroth you in righteousness and justice, in love and compassion*" (Hos. 2:19).

❦

The war is over forty days long now. Soon it will be fifty.

❦

The war is almost sixty days long. Soon it will be seventy.

❦

The war is almost one hundred days long.

❦

The war is over two hundred days long.

❦

The war is over three hundred days long.

❧

The war is almost a year long.

❧

The war is over a year long.

❧

Around the 250th day of the war, a friend held out a dog tag with a piece of masking tape. It recorded the 151st day of the war. "Is this yours?" he asked. It was mine. I misplaced it and replaced it months ago. It is light and cheap but felt heavy in my hand. I thought by now the war would be over. But a hundred days after I lost that dog tag, we are still counting.

❧

I try to create a window of time every day to do something proactive. Every morning when I wake up, I will drop an email to my representative in Congress. I will then reach out to an Israeli friend with a text and a virtual hug. I will write an article.

My strategy: If I block out times on a schedule, I will give the war a dedicated, limited space and prevent it from finding its way into every crevice, creating paralyzing turmoil.

It hasn't worked. The war has crept into every crevice.

❧

Over time, as this war persists or any other societal ill continues – as it will – it's normal, I read, to lose energy, have difficulty focusing or maintaining routine, have difficulty eating or feel guilty experiencing even small pleasure when hostages, civilians, or soldiers are suffering.

I notice how little music I listen to. I haven't seen a movie in months.

The Talmud amplifies feelings of discomfort around personal enjoyment when it states: "When the community is immersed in suffering, a person may not say: 'I will go to my home and I will eat and drink, and peace be upon you, my soul.'"[45]

A Theology of Distraction

After his wife died, C. S. Lewis in *A Grief Observed* wrote that he could not write or read a letter. "Even shaving. What does it matter now whether my cheek is rough or smooth? They say an unhappy man wants distractions – something to take him out of himself."[46] Lewis understood that we need distractions to live. We need to recover that little spark in ourselves when we stop thinking about one thing or stop thinking altogether.

※

Forgetting, even for a few minutes, allows us that recovery. I escape into a novel, binge watch, or have a drink with a friend. I eat. I eat to forget.

※

The snacks are ruining me.

※

But sometimes I cannot find distraction anywhere. I dare not even look for it. I wonder how anyone can experience joy and lightness when there are babies in captivity.

Who am I to have a snack?

❧

I look up the definition of snack. "A snack is a small portion of food generally eaten between meals. Snacks come in a variety of forms including packaged snack foods and other processed foods, as well as items made from fresh ingredients at home."

"Snack foods are typically designed to be portable, quick, and satisfying."[47]

❧

My portions are not small. I am not satisfied. The cravings I experience are not physical. They are a great gaping maw of a hunger for wholeness that food will never satisfy.

❧

Are the hostages given snacks? I cannot help wondering if their days resemble mine in any way. Then I whisk this absurd question from my mind.

❧

One member of our visiting group says that he is in Israel to visit his brothers and sisters who are broken. An Israeli accompanying our group whispers in my ear, "He does not understand. Our government may be broken. Our hearts may be broken. But we are not broken."

She is rightfully offended.

Morning Has Broken

❧

The Tnuva cottage cheese container in Israel is stamped "Bring Them Home" in Hebrew and English.

A small egg is imprinted with the words *Am Yisrael Chai* – the nation of Israel lives – in spidery faded blue letters.

I have seen *Am Yisrael Chai* everywhere, but this is the first time I've seen it on an egg.

I cannot distract myself from this war if the cottage cheese and the eggs also protest. It's an alternate breakfast of champions.

❧

The simple egg has an important role in Jewish tradition. In the Talmud, the volume size of an egg serves as one of the few paradigmatic measures of food consumption. It is eaten by the mourner at the darkest hour because its shape represents the circle of life. Its content is the ultimate symbol of life. It suggests possibility.

❧

I call my sister in Jerusalem who says, "Over there, to live you have to remind yourself what's happening. Over here, to live you have to forget what's happening."

❧

In the book of Ecclesiastes, we are told seven times to eat and be merry because these small, temporal happinesses are a gift from God. The biblical cynic who told us all is futile, and there's nothing new under the sun also told us to enjoy the fleeting moments of pleasure God has given us as a drop of psychic relief. Indulge in those moments. God has created that wisp of joy, too.

Sometimes the mandate to eat, drink, and be merry in the book follows immediately after the conclusion that the wicked sometimes thrive and the righteous sometimes suffer.

This is emotional whiplash.

This is life.

I eat and drink with friends. Pleasure is not trivial. It is Godly.

※

There are relationship experts who believe that distraction is essential when managing irreconcilable differences. If you love someone long enough, you will continue to have a version of the same argument forever. Every anniversary is a celebration of all the years you've had the same argument.

※

When you know you're about to hit that hard place where nothing yields, be smart. Go bowling. Jump in a pool together. Go to the supermarket together. Buy the best pint of ice cream you can find and then eat it out of the container in the parking lot.

Distracting myself, I've decided, is not being intellectually dishonest. It is being emotionally honest.

There are some things we are always going to fight about. That's when we need to remember why we also love one another.

※

As a diverse people, we are always going to fight. But we need to stop on occasion to sing together, to march down the streets together, to pray and sway together, to cry together, and to remember that we also love one another.

Sitting Down with God

Distraction also helps me manage a persistent problem with activism: compassion fatigue. It's the side-effect of giving to a cause or to others who are suffering that encompasses all of our emotional, physical, and spiritual distress. It can manifest as the dark cloud of burnout, depression, anxiety. It can also become secondary traumatic stress that protestors carry because of closely aligning with the cause and those who are carrying its primary pain.

※

I scour websites to educate myself on the signs: decreased engagement in work or in class. The inability to start or complete tasks and assignments. Less productivity. More guilt, irritability, and moodiness. Withdrawal from social circles or normal social activities. Decreased interaction with close friends. Poor self-care. Nightmares. Bad sleep patterns or little sleep. Heightened blame or judgment of others who are complacent or less engaged with the cause.

These symptoms can exacerbate if the work is protracted and those experiencing the stress are under-supported or lack the human and financial resources to do the work properly.

It is challenging right now to have the bandwidth for those with whom I have weak ties – acquaintances or relatives in my outer circle. I am wary of compromising relationships that are important. Those relationships are crucial to my health and well-being. My people always keep me grounded when the floor beneath my feet crumbles.

I go to the doctor. He asks me how my family in Israel is. He visited the country ten days before the war broke out. "You have a beautiful country," he says to me. "I have never seen more patriotism. But there is hate everywhere. Maybe we have forgotten how to be human."

We talk for longer than we've ever talked. Then he says, "I've taken care of you for a long time now. I have never seen you this sad."

I came to talk to him about the pounding sadness. I am not myself. He tells me that when he was ten, his father died. He has not been himself since. He cannot go to funerals because for two weeks afterward, he loses the capacity to do anything. He advises me to slow down, to exercise more, to eat better. Every obvious thing I could have told you he would say he says, but he says it with the kindest eyes. Then he offers advice that is not medical.

"If you sit down long enough, you can look up at God."

Sleep for the Weary

I dream about sleep.

❦

Oliver Sacks calls music that repeats itself in your head on an endless loop a brainworm.[48] It wriggles in the ear and stays for a while. My brainworm plays one song in C minor throughout the night hours. "*Acheinu kol beit Yisrael…*" When the song is over, I loop it again. "Our brothers and sisters – the whole house of Israel – who are in trouble or captivity, on the sea or dry land…"

Then, in Jerusalem, I am leaning against a wall a few feet from the parents of a hostage who is now missing his left arm, and those in the room begin this song that asks for God's mercy. Bring those in distress from darkness to light speedily and soon.

I turn into the wall to cry because who am I to cry in front of them? It is no longer the distant brother or a sister across an ocean. It is a son.

❦

Morning Has Broken

I overhear a student shuffling out of an assembly say to a friend, "I can't sing *Acheinu* one more time." My first reaction is offense. I hold my breath. What do you mean you cannot sing this song when people are still trapped in darkness? Then I exhale and realize that forty days of the same song and the same problem can get musically arduous. We need a longer playlist of doom. Let there be a playlist of consolation.

✎

My clothes are on a chair in the night in case another siren goes off, in which case we'll evacuate to the stairwells. In the south and the north – even near the beautiful beaches of Tel Aviv and Herzliya – rockets illuminate the night sky. The firework display of malice looks monstrously beautiful in that brief moment before I remind myself what a rocket explosion actually is. Maybe small children from Sderot found the sky mesmerizing before they were evacuated. Theirs are rocket lives. The sirens form the playlist of their childhoods.

✎

For the first month of the war, sleep came to me in snatches or not at all, interrupted by what I thought were nightmares but were simply a constant loop of actual images – photos of shoes trapped in pools of blood and rubble like insects trapped in amber. Small children alive in cages. Babies burned to death. I try not to watch the videos of masked martyrs jumping on pick-up trucks and waving flags, pulling the hair of a young woman captive. I cannot unsee what I have seen.

✎

Later, there will be forty-three minutes of visual testimony to show to journalists and politicians to tell the world to look. Seeing must be believing. So few believe us. Even after they see.

✎

Maybe it is a mitzva to look because once we look, we cannot say nothing. We cannot do nothing.

I understand why people ignore wars and turn to the section of the paper with lots of numbers, sports news, or the latest hair care products. They cannot look straight at war. If they don't see it, it has not happened. The savagery of war is deadening. And so, I cannot sleep.

※

Who am I to complain about sleep? I am not in the killing fields of Gaza or on the border of Lebanon.

※

I speak to a friend who has several sons in the war. I tell him I feel guilty. He reminds me that during wartime whatever we do, we feel guilty for all we are not doing. His son, a reservist who was sent to the north, feels guilty that he was not in the south. His son who is in the south feels guilty that someone he knows has been injured, but he returned home whole. Even the wounded feel guilty about still being alive when others are dead.

Throughout the Talmud we read that all of Israel is responsible, one for the other. Maybe this blanket of guilt is another way of expressing our covenantal bondedness to each other.

※

Guilt interrupts my sleep.

※

At the age of forty-four, Zev Jabotinsky came to America to raise funds for the Zionist cause. The year was 1940, eight years before Israel became a state. He arrived at the Revisionist Zionist camp in Hunter, N.Y. He was exhausted from running himself ragged to support the idea of Israel.

He laid down on a bed, and a doctor came into his room, and Jabotinsky whispered, "I am so tired. I am so tired." And those are the last words that Jabotinsky ever said.[49]

The Nursery

The news broadcasts a photo of a table in a nursery in Kibbutz Be'eri. Soldiers left a sign apologizing that they broke into the greenhouses to water the plants. The kibbutz members who returned expected all the plants to be dead. But now some of them are still alive.

Soldiers, for a few minutes, became gardeners. To grow new life in a war. That is the hardest thing.

❧

I will not forget the kindnesses that happen even in battle.

❧

Long ago, the prophet Jeremiah told his people in captivity that they must become gardeners. "Thus said God of Hosts, the God of Israel, to the whole community that I exiled from Jerusalem to Babylon: Build houses and live in them, plant gardens and eat their fruit" (Jer. 29:4–5).

❧

Plant and bring life to exile so that you can have a life after exile.

Rolling in Its Dust

"Great sages," Maimonides wrote, "would kiss the borders of the Land, kiss its stones, and roll in its dust. Similarly, Psalms 102:15 declares: 'Behold, your servants hold her stones dear and cherish her dust.'"[50]

◆

I hold tight to a mental postcard from the eighth chapter of Deuteronomy: "For the Lord your God is bringing you into a good land – a land with streams and pools of water, with springs flowing in the valleys and hills; a land with wheat and barley, vines and fig trees, pomegranates, olive oil, and honey; a land where bread will not be scarce and you will lack nothing; a land where the rocks are iron and you can dig copper out of the hills" (Deut. 8:7–9).

You will lack nothing. That's what the Good Book says.

On a dark, dark day, twenty-one soldiers were killed by the collapse of a building in Gaza; it was the highest number of soldiers killed on a single day of the war's first hundred days. I go back to Deuteronomy 8 to try to remember why this place is worth fighting for. One day we will lack nothing. Peace alone would give us everything.

❧

"*If* I forget thee, O Jerusalem…"

It's always the "if" that gets me. If. If. If. What *if* there were real peace, and we could put all the bloodshed and the tears behind us?

❧

Two weeks after my first trip, I touch down in Tel Aviv again. This time, it is not the captain who thanks us for flying but a stewardess. She ends flatly: "We wish for more peaceful days soon. Shalom." We are normalizing war as a condition of being. The first time, the captain was so grateful we were going to Israel. The person who checked our passports could not believe we would visit during a war. Why come for a visit during the war? We are coming because of the war. Now, the war is where we are. We fly into it as if today were any other day.

❧

Hatikva asks not only that we have a country but also that we be free in our own land. You can be in your own land and not be free there.

When we stop worrying about the South, we worry about the North. We worry all the time about everywhere.

If good fences make good neighbors, what happens when the fences have been destroyed?

❧

Before I built a wall, I'd ask to know
What I was walling in or walling out,
And to whom I was like to give offense.
Something there is that doesn't love a wall,
That wants it down.[51]

Morning Has Broken

❧

When this war is over, the walls will be higher. Some of them will be real walls. Others will be the walls of the mind. No trespassing, our hearts will say to strangers. These fences will not make us better neighbors. They will only heighten the growing distance. There will be no curiosity to know what's on the other side of the wall.

Maya's Braid

Those from the envelope of kibbutzim and small towns that border Gaza are housed in hotels around the country. Families cannot grieve at home. Instead, they grieve everywhere. The loss of a son, a daughter, a grandmother. The loss of security. The loss of leadership. There is so much to grieve. Where does one even begin?

Everywhere there are red and black photos of the kidnapped. Age 24. Age 72. Age 4. Honor the singularity of grief, I tell myself. The hostages are a group, but they are also not a group.

Every person is a universe. Last night, a history teacher was killed. He once taught the son of a friend.

⚘

I focus on Maya Goren's face.

I stare at the thick grey braid that wraps around her neck over her left shoulder. She is a kindergarten teacher in Kibbutz Nir Oz. Her nephew, Amir, said she was organizing her classroom when Hamas abducted her. Her husband Avner was home at the time. The terrorists killed him. She has four children a little younger than mine – 18, 21, 23, and 25. Maya's mother, who lives in the center of Israel, is waiting for news about her daughter. Maya's children are in a hotel in Eilat. They buried a father and wait for news of their mother.

Maya is 56.

I am 57.

✥

Compound mourning overwhelms, and it is impossible to focus on one face in prayer. If the heart can break one hundred times, it can break 240 times.

✥

I walk down the long corridor at Ben Gurion Airport to leave again. The faces of all those kidnapped are still sitting at the nexus of the floor and wall. Some have been blessedly removed. I read each name and age – 24. 4. 19. 72. 61. It took me a long time to get to the gate. Goodbye, Maya.

I didn't want to leave her. And then I left her.

✥

In New York days later, I see Maya Goren's face on a kidnapped poster framed in red. She has followed me here. I say an awkward hello to her braid. Please help bring her home alive, the poster asks. Of course. Just tell me what I can do. I'll do anything.

✥

Months later, a few minutes before Shabbat descends, I learn that Maya Goren was murdered.

✥

That beautiful braid will soon decompose in Gaza.

Bring her home so that her children may bury her with dignity.

❧

In late July 2023, Maya's corpse was rescued and brought back to Kibbutz Nir Oz. She was buried next to Avner. A few days later, a photo surfaces that pre-dates October 7th of Maya feeding Kfir Bibas, the sweet, red-headed baby whose fate is as yet undetermined. Kfir looks up lovingly at Maya, who is holding him in a tight embrace and feeding him something white and undiscernible with a teaspoon.

❧

I leave Israel again on the fiftieth day of the war. There are black and red signs everywhere that say "50 Days in Hell." The Hebrew for hell is *Gehinom*, named after the valley in Jerusalem where child sacrifices were conducted by a wicked, foreign tribe.

❧

Maybe there will come a time in Ben Gurion Airport when there will be more spaces than posters and then no posters at all.

❧

Walking in Jerusalem, I almost trip on the back of a stroller and wonder who would leave a stroller on a median. As I get closer, I see that it has been left there intentionally. The stroller is a protest.

On the seat is a photo of Kfir, the youngest of the thirty-two children taken hostage. He was nine-months old at the time. He will remember nothing of this, but it will live within him nevertheless.

Morning Has Broken

❦

Thomas Hand was told his nine-year-old daughter Emily was dead. He mourned her until the day he was told that she was a hostage, and she would be released.

When he hugged her for the first time, he told the press, he probably squeezed her too hard.

She thought she'd been gone a year.

"Last night she cried until her face was red and blotchy, she couldn't stop. She didn't want any comfort; I guess she's forgotten how to be comforted," Tom said. All he wants to do is protect her now. Be her shadow. Never let her out of his sight.

Emily lost her mother to cancer when she was two.

"She's a very determined little girl, very strong, I knew that her spirit would get her through it."[52]

❦

Hannah Katzir, a cancer survivor in her seventies from Kibbutz Nir Oz, can now include in her life resume that she is also a survivor of terrorism. Her family was also told she died. But she was released.

❦

Terror undermines the belief you are fated to contentment. There can be, in this climate, no truly happy endings.

❦

Further down the street in Jerusalem, a few blocks past the stroller, is a carousel, filled with empty wooden horses with their stiff, colorful tails and tresses.

Sad carnival music plays as the horses spin and wait for children.

Faith and Doubt

I first encountered Saadia Gaon's *Emunot veDe'ot*, Beliefs and Opinions, when I was eighteen. I have turned to part seven of his introduction many times in my life, both to legitimate the role of doubt as a believer and to interrogate my own reasons for doubt when they arise. I do this to check that my doubts are neither overly academic nor spiritually lazy.

~

Saadia Gaon enumerates eight insufficient reasons for doubt that he has observed in the world.

~

1) The first reason for doubt is that people are normally reluctant to think about issues that require depth. They believe the truth is bitter and, therefore, run away from it. Should they run away from anything difficult in the material world of work, they would be unable to sustain themselves.

2) The second reason for doubt is stupidity and the valorization of idleness. Ignorance was not bliss to Saadia Gaon.

3) The third reason for doubt is that an individual expends so much effort on worldly matters that he or she has no time to think.

4) The fourth reason for doubt is that a person displays too little reflection or too much indifference when an idea is presented.

5) The fifth reason for doubt is arrogance. The know-it-all believes there is nothing more to know on a subject than what he already knows.

6) The sixth reason for doubt is that a convincing and persuasive unbeliever poisons the faith of a believer, who generally protects himself from the heat and cold but fails to protect his faith from unwanted exposure.

7) The seventh reason for doubt is that an unconvincing believer offers a weak argument for his faith that turns off the doubter and makes belief into an object of ridicule.

8) The eighth reason for doubt is that a person subjectively hates a believer and, therefore, hates the God of the believer.

❧

Saadia Gaon, in a few short pages, offers shades of doubt that he believes reflect undue subjectivity, material excess, or intellectual indolence. But if a believer begins to doubt because his prayers and requests go unanswered, or he observes the wicked enjoying themselves or the just suffering, or if people die indiscriminately, there is a place for doubt. Read on. Saadia Gaon has legitimized doubt and invited us to continue.

❧

My prayers have gone unanswered. I have seen the wicked celebrate. I have seen the righteous suffer. I have witnessed people die indiscriminately. I have continued reading. And here is what I also learned that is not from a page of medieval Jewish philosophy....

My prayers are also answered. The wicked are also punished. The righteous are also joyous. And so many children are born, and so many who are sick are healed.

The Maternity Ward

In Egypt, way back in the days of Moses, after all the infertility in Genesis, we became a people of substance. This made Pharaoh anxious: "And he said to his people, 'Look, the Israelite people are much too numerous for us'" (Ex. 1:9). It is unusual to complain about a Jewish population explosion.

Pharaoh tried to break us. But the more he afflicted us, the more we propagated. It says so right in the Bible: "The more they were oppressed, the more they increased and spread out…" (Ex. 1:12).

It's counterintuitive to suffer and grow. But it happens. Persecution should lead to human shrinkage. No one wants to bring children into generations of slavery unless belief in a future of freedom is strong.

Almost eighteen thousand babies were born in Israel during the first weeks of the war. Many of them were named after kibbutzim or hostages. Their names will carry the memory of this time long past this time.

Every child is an affirmation of faith.

>8<

When they persecute us, we will reproduce.

>8<

We may be small, but we are not insignificant.

>8<

One day those who hate us will see that the best way to fight a war is in the maternity ward.

One Day

At a rally, against a jewel-blue sky, I stand alone for a few minutes amidst the crowd from Texas, Chicago, New Jersey, and Boston. The singer gets on stage and sways with his back-up singers. The National Mall suddenly thrums with tens of thousands singing in unison.

> *In this maze, you can lose your way, your way*
> *It might drive you crazy*
> *But don't let it faze you, no way, no way*
> *Sometimes in my tears I drown (I drown)*
> *But I never let it get me down (get me down)*
> *So when negativity surrounds (surrounds)*
> *I know someday, it'll all turn around because*
> *All my life, I've been waitin' for (waitin' for)*
> *I've been prayin' for (prayin' for), for the people to say*
> *That we don't wanna fight no more (fight no more)*
> *There'll be no more wars (no more wars), and our children will play*
> *One day (one day), one day (one day)*
> *One day (oh, oh, oh, oh-oh-oh, one day)*
> *One day (one day), one day (one day)*
> *One day (oh-oh-oh)*[53]

At first, I refuse to sing. I tell myself it is inappropriate. This is not a concert. We must chant and shout. We must permit nothing less than red-hot anger.

Then I look around me, at so many students, our gorgeous future, with their eyes closed and their mouths wide open, singing their hope into existence. And I join them. I am not alone. We are not alone. My mouth opens, and the lyrics fly high up past the signs and flags into that blue, blue sky.

※

In the middle of the night, two words replay in my brain. One day. One day. One day.

※

"We can't be sure, can hardly guess how history's arc will bend," writes philosopher Kieran Setiya in *Life is Hard*. "And so we cannot say what human life means, if it means anything at all. The question that remains is what to feel when so much is unknown… Should we be lifted by hope or flattened by despair?"[54]

※

I have been flattened by despair. I choose to be lifted by hope. Hope is a choice.

The Last Normal Day

I cannot remember the last normal day.

✎

I try to imagine a future normal day, but I find it hard to plan beyond twelve-hour increments.[55]

✎

Jews love to count. Numbers are part of all our stories. But now, the act of counting that stretches close to a year seems ugly and reckless.

✎

My imagination bends toward horror these days. Reality, it turns out, is worse than my imagination.

✎

On the eighty-third day of the war, the Israeli papers report six thousand military injuries, five hundred soldier deaths. We reached an unbearable milestone in this war. Wait, the number just changed in the past few minutes to 501. The number of soldiers who died in ground operations in Gaza is 167. Add that to the number of civilians killed on October 7th and the hostages who have died in captivity, and the numbers have reached a quadrant of incomprehensibility.

On October 7th itself, 704 soldiers were killed. Sixty-three police officers died that day. On *Yom Ha-Zikaron* of 2024, the Defense Ministry reported the deaths of 716 soldiers. Included in that number were 39 local security officers, 68 police officers, and six members of the Shin Bet. That makes, in total, on this Memorial Day in Israel, 25,040 people who have died serving the country since 1860, when we started counting.

※

We are not finished counting. Just look at the empty spaces being cleared in military cemeteries.

※

Today, someone sends another video fragment of a soldier turning the corner of a building in a Gaza ruin and shooting. Stop. Please stop.

We see too much of war. We know too much. We are not meant to know this much. In other wars, civilians did not know this much.

Also, we know very little.

We know enough to talk incessantly but not enough to understand anything.

※

In the morning, I rush to check the names of Israeli soldiers who died while I was asleep in America. It is getting worse. Every day, there are three or five. On harsher weekends there are eleven or fourteen. In their headshots, most are wearing helmets. This is all most of us will ever know of any one of them – a name, a city, and a visual memento, only shared on the day each died.

Some soldiers smile at the person behind a lens a few feet away as if it's a perfectly normal time to take a photo. To see the smile of a young man already dead seems like a betrayal of the beautiful tomorrow that soldier could have had in another lifetime. Susan Sontag understood: "To take a photograph is to participate in another person's mortality, vulnerability, mutability. Precisely by slicing out this moment and freezing it, all photographs testify to time's relentless melt."[56]

We have become obsessed with these photos. "Needing to have reality confirmed and experience enhanced by photographs is an aesthetic consumerism to which everyone is now addicted. Industrial societies turn their citizens into image-junkies; it is the most irresistible form of mental pollution."[57]

֎

I release my breath into a sigh when I recognize no names. But what difference? They are all our brothers and sisters, sons and daughters. Still, it makes a difference. The suffering creeps closer and closer. No fortress can hold it at bay long enough so it will not breach the thin defense of human consciousness.

֎

My nephew, an officer in *Otef Aza*, the Gaza Envelope, sends me a photo of himself in uniform reunited with his younger daughter. His eyes are closed as this little angel of a girl puts her sweet, innocent head on his strong, olive-green shoulder. In my mind, her head smells like baby shampoo and breakfast cereal.

The front door is in the background. Always there are front doors opening in photos and videos and gapes of delighted surprise when a solider comes home. Children hang on the legs of fathers. Wives and husbands embrace and cry. What a relief it must be to see love on the other side of the door, even if only for a day.

But there are no photos of fathers and mothers who just wait on the other side of the door or wait by the window like Sisera's mother. They await the knock that may or may not come. It can be one of two kinds of knocks.

※

A friend sends a photo of a high-ranking officer who has not been home in eighty-three days. He, too, smiles. Maybe he forgot the smell of his wife's perfume or the softness of his mattress at home and what it is like to wake up late one morning just because.

※

In other photos, important people from other countries who drop in for a visit stand near tunnels in flak jackets. They look serious. The tunnel is deep, sometimes stories deep. It connects to other tunnels creating an alternate underground labyrinth of dread. There is a universe underneath the surface of our universe that waits to live above the surface. It is a dark, secret, powerful universe we will neither know nor imagine.

※

I often entertain myself by constructing imaginary lives for people I've never met. Just give me the window of a beautiful house lit at night, and I'll assemble a whole family who lives there in minutes.

Now the stories I fabricate have no old uncle who won a lottery and blew the money on ten pink Cadillacs or a sister trapped in a loveless marriage to a man who inherited a fortune. They are stories of tired young women in combat units hungry to see their nieces and nephews again. They are the stories of hostages stuck in a tunnel somewhere. But these stories go nowhere because I cannot imagine any details. I do not know this underground world at all.

Regret

It's late Friday afternoon in the United States. More bad news: three hostages who escaped were killed by friendly fire, a detestable expression that dishonors the seriousness of the mistake.

There is nothing friendly about gunfire.

I walk into the sanctuary to welcome in Shabbat but am too unfocused. The families of those three did their own praying and wishing and hoping to see a son, a father, a brother come home. Those three men found a way out. They risked their lives for their freedom. Shot by their own, they escaped but could not escape. They were free and then not free.

❧

In A. B. Yehoshua's novel *Friendly Fire*. Yirmiyahu, one of the central characters, loses his wife to cancer. He also loses a son to friendly fire. He leaves Israel and moves to East Africa. When his sister-in-law, Daniela, comes to visit him on Chanukah, he tosses the Israeli newspapers she brings him into the fire along with the gift of candles for the menora. He has had enough. He needs no reminders of Israeli news or holidays.

> Here there are no ancient graves and no floor tiles from a destroyed synagogue; no museum with a fragment of a burnt Torah; no testimonies about pogroms and the Holocaust. There's no exile here, no Diaspora... There's no struggle between tradition and revolution. No rebellion against the forefathers and no new interpretations. No one feels compelled to decide if he is a Jew or an Israeli or maybe a Canaanite, or if the state is more democratic or more Jewish, if there's hope for it or if it's done for. The people around me are free and clear of that whole exhausting and confusing tangle. But life goes on. I am seventy years old, Daniela, and I am permitted to let go.[58]

I find no fault in the imaginary Yirmiyahu who leaves Israel because his imaginary son was killed by friendly fire. Identity fatigue closed in on him, and he sought a getaway car. In the wilds of Africa, he will not reclaim his wife or his son. He will be momentarily distracted by a different view.

※

It's not clear how these young soldiers who shot three hostages will work through the boulder-heavy regret. A mother of one hostage forgives. Iris Haim exonerates the IDF for the death of her son Yotam. She heard that morale was low in the army after the deaths of the three, so she sent a message to the Bislamach Brigade's 17th Battalion, which was responsible. Was she angry? "Not for one minute. There was pain, there was sadness, there was huge sadness about the fact that Yotam isn't here, and we were in shock, total shock, but we weren't angry."

She consoled them. "I know that everything that happened is absolutely not your fault, and nobody's fault except that of Hamas.... And don't hesitate for a second if you see a terrorist.... Don't think that you killed a hostage deliberately. You have to look after yourselves because that's the only way can you look after us."[59]

If only one story of forgiveness existed in the world, it would be this.

※

After the Yom Kippur War, even Golda Meir's critics understood that, despite the significant number of military casualties, she had ensured an eventual victory. "From a military perspective, the war ended well for Israel… Nevertheless, Golda considered the war a spectacular failure."[60] Though the commission of inquiry absolved her of all responsibility, no one was surprised by her subsequent decision to step down from office. Her leadership days were over. Years later, before her death, Golda acknowledged that since that war, "I am not the same person."[61]

※

The very first law that Maimonides codifies in his "Laws of Repentance" discusses the essential nature of regret in the process of change: "How does one confess? He states: 'I implore You, God, I sinned, I transgressed, I committed iniquity before You by doing the following. Behold, *I regret and am embarrassed for my deeds.* I promise never to repeat this act again.'"[62]

Regret makes us into different people. I am not the same person. Maybe I am worse. Maybe I am better. It depends on what I do with my regrets.

※

Friday night after the hostages were killed by their own, my tears flowed in the pews. "My eyes are spent with tears. My heart is in tumult. My being melts away over the ruin of my poor people…" (Lam. 2:11).

I hope, dear God, the tears are enough tonight. I have no words to sing to you. I am not sure where You are right now, but I am searching for You. Somewhere in the rubble of this war lies my faith.

Do You see it?

Morning Has Broken

※

A woman waits until the crowd thins to speak with me. "I do not know where God is. I cannot figure this out. I do not know what to think." She is embarrassed.

There is a question in this statement. Can you tell me where God is?

Please do not ask me this question. I do not know why this happened. It is unfair and unjust and tragic. There are no simple answers. There are no answers. That does not stop us from asking. I am only human so I ask. I am only human, so I expect no answers. I bristle at people who claim they have answers.

Instead, I tell her a Hasidic story.

A poor man leaves his family, spends the rest of his savings, and takes a wagon to see his Rebbe several day's journey away. The years have not been good to our poor man, who has made bad financial decisions and suffered a spate of family tragedies. The poor man must travel to his Rebbe, who surely knows why these bad things have happened to him and can explain.

The poor man waits in the hall and then is finally allowed into the Rebbe's chambers. He stands on the other side of the Rebbe's wide desk and unwinds his string of distress. The Rebbe says nothing. The quiet is agonizing. Was this worth the poor man's last rubles, this journey to silence? Suddenly, the Rebbe gets up and walks to the other side of the desk and puts his arm around the poor man. In a whisper he says, "I cannot explain why any of this happened to you. But I can stand beside you in your pain."

※

We cannot understand. We can, however, stand beside those in pain.

※

Braided in the anguish is the tenderness of company.

※

Rena's story is awash with gentleness. She spoke, signed her book for me, and thanked me for "coming to Israel and giving us *chizuk*." Strength. This makes no sense. I gave her no strength and no story. She gave me her strength and her story. Unlike my imaginary plots and characters, her stories are constructed of facts and memories. On the first page, she is nine years old and dying under a tree in Bergen-Belsen. A tree in a concentration camp? Bergen-Belsen seems like a place vacant of a tree's beauty. My grandmother has been dead for over ten years. I can no longer verify the existence of trees in Bergen-Belsen.

Suddenly people are shouting to Rena, "*Ihr seid frei* – you are free." The English army arrived. Food and medical help were on the way. Rena did not understand. She was too sick and too tired to move. All she wanted was her mother.[63] She was all alone in the world. She, too, was free and not free.

Six mothers raised Rena, one woman after another, conceiving and birthing her, hiding her, nursing her back to health, adopting her, and teaching her. One day in her new school in America, Rena's teacher told the class to make cards for their mothers. It was soon to be Mother's Day. But which of her mothers should Rena make a card for, she wondered?

"The issue is that I've already had so many mothers. In the past, every time I got a new mother, I lost her. Most of my mothers are dead."[64]

※

Rena speaks to us in the basement conference room of a hotel in Jerusalem about all her mothers. Then the story changes to those she's mothered. She has over forty great-grandchildren now. Twelve are serving in the IDF – in this war. You were freed, Rena, to be a mother in Israel, just like Deborah in the Bible. All of your children know that they have only one mother, the matriarch of a new, beautiful tribe, who, on that day when the English army arrived, had a whisper of hope. Now, Rena, you have a small army of your own.

Rena dedicated her book to her parents, to the ones who gave birth to her and the ones who raised her.

⁂

The dedication in a book of new essays I've just opened today reads: "This book is dedicated to Zoloft."[65]

I laugh. And I remember that I used to laugh more.

⁂

Rena asks if she can stay to hear the next speakers. Jon and Rachel Goldberg-Polin are the parents of a hostage – a young man who was supposed to be traveling the world creating his own stories. Rena's suffering is behind her. Let us hope. The suffering of these parents is in front of them every minute and beneath their eyelids at night. It's been more than two weeks since they heard from him.

⁂

As the war continues, the clarity we expected about its end is the size of a grain of rice. The halcyon days of sitting in cafés and shooting the breeze with friends are impossibly far away. We watch our hopes for peace float away like a red balloon released accidently into the sky.

⁂

From the corner of my eye, I spot a photo on the wall of an American airport. A war veteran wears a T-shirt that says, "Be Excellent to Others." My standards these days are lower. Be Kind. If you cannot Be

Kind, Be Decent. If you cannot Be Decent, then just leave everybody alone.

⁂

On October 22, 2023, someone submitted a new verb to the Urban Dictionary: Israeled.

Definition: "When someone asks you for sharing something of yours and then fight you to get you out of it. And tell everyone you took it from them." This makes no sense. The English is terrible. People heard about it. They wrote in. The administrators changed the definition, but they kept the word.

On July 8, 2020, another submission defined "jew" as a verb: "To hoard money, and even if you have a lot of money, you're really cheap, acting as if you barely have any. When friends ask you for money, you don't give them any, and when you have to go somewhere, you'll barely scrape enough change together to afford it, even though you've got plenty of money."[66]

No one took this definition down.

We cannot allow language to fail us.

It's time to write another letter.

Blessed Is the Judge

It is hard to dedicate focused attention to personal problems while this war is going on. Young children will still fall, scrape knees, and cry for parents. Teenagers will still storm out of rooms thinking no one understands. Adults will lose jobs, get sick, and have their hearts broken. Any bad news in addition to the war is crushing – like a pyramid of trouble with the war at its base.

꽃

My mother-in-law is very ill. She was taken to the hospital in Israel on October 7th. The heart has enough chambers to let in more grief. She is in pain. She is afraid. Everyone else is also afraid but for other reasons.

꽃

A Muslim friend and cleric reached out to ask how I am. I tell him about the way the war is wrecking my people. He knows. But I need to tell him again, in my own way, or I will be guilty of hiding something that is consuming me.

I also tell him that my mother-in-law is very ill. I do not know why it is important for him to know. Maybe I want him to understand what loss on top of loss is and to judge me and my people favorably. Maybe I am just grateful that someone who is not one of my people cares. A few days later, he tells me he recited a special prayer of healing for my mother-in-law. I am grateful. He reminds me that we are all still part of a human family.

Thank you, Mohamed.

⁂

Weeks later, I got an email from a Presbyterian Teaching Elder and professor of Bible:

> *Please know that my tears are flowing even as my prayers ascend to God on behalf of Israel. May He wield his sword of justice against this modern-day incarnation of the Amalekites, and may He bear his balm of comfort in the face of such sorrow and suffering. Please be assured that, despite media to the contrary, many of us do love and stand with you. So sorry for what you all are going through. So heart-breaking.*

⁂

We have friends. Language fails us, but sometimes it befriends us.

⁂

I visit Shalva, a campus in Jerusalem dedicated to special needs children. A father in a black suit and hat tells us he is a social worker from Ashkelon whose family now lives in a hotel nearby with hundreds of other evacuees. He goes to Ashkelon each day. There has never been more work. He pushes his son in a wheelchair while his other children hang on both arms. Thank goodness for Shalva, he tells us. Their large family is stuck in one hotel room. They appreciate all the kindnesses, but it is hard.

Now, his son with special needs blessedly has somewhere to go for a few hours. We tour a storeroom with a month of supplies: canned food, mattresses, oxygen. Each floor must have a secure room in the event of an attack. Moving children in braces and wheelchairs down the stairs is nearly impossible when a siren goes off with only a minute and a half to prepare.

The children and younger adults dance with us in the cafeteria. Loudly, they sing Rebbe Nachman's song: "The whole world is a very narrow bridge. But the main thing is not to be afraid." Rebbe Nachman did not write this song for this very day. He wrote it to give an ounce of courage to himself or someone else on another day, centuries ago, when there was a different reason to be afraid.

※

Wars end. That's what the history books say. The Franco-Prussian War ended. The American Revolution ended. The Civil War ended. World War I ended. World War II ended. The Korean War ended. The Vietnam War ended. These are wars that lasted for years.

We cannot afford a war that lasts for years.

※

Right now, the official count of Palestinian dead number over forty thousand. It is unclear where these numbers come from. Others throw out the number seventeen thousand. Thousands are terrorists. Thousands are not. The numbers are not exact – the margin of error is not a margin – the number is unbearable. Thousands died from failure to evacuate. Thousands were used by Hamas as civilian shields and decoys. Thousands were casualties of war. The survivors, too, cannot afford a war that lasts for years. The loss of life is staggering. God "showers compassion on all His creations" (Ps. 145:9), and so must we. When Jews use unspeakable language about civilians as a group, I see their souls shrivel.

※

Someone, somewhere will one day wave a white flag of surrender. Or a general will admit defeat. Or one final battle will determine the outcome.

Grim men around polished conference tables will negotiate terms. Reparations will be determined. Admissions and confessions will be extracted. Mistakes were made. Plans for rebuilding will be touted. Other countries will be asked to contribute to the reconstruction funds. Promises will be made to clear the debris, erect new and improved cities, and design roads better than the ones destroyed.

All of the sentences above are in the passive tense, as if after a war agency and responsibility have been removed from those who carried out past actions and vaguely placed on others to clear the debris.

☙

Wars do not end in a day. They unravel. They linger like chronic illnesses.

☙

Dates, however, will one day be solidified for the history books. The war started on October 7th. It ended on…

☙

I can make no prediction. I can imagine no future that is empty of this conflict. That is the paucity of my imagination.

☙

I ask friends, the parents of several soldiers, how they are doing. "We all have been learning to get used to a very difficult situation, and we work on our courage and patience, and on finding strong coping mechanisms," one writes. "We have ups and downs – lots of bad news in and out of our community, some days it seems too heavy to hold. But our people are strong, and it certainly helps that we are in this together, with a lot of heroism and kindness."

They work on their own courage and patience. They treasure heroism and kindness. I wonder if the coping mechanisms ever stop working.

※

"It's very nice to say, 'And if you will it, it is no dream,' as Herzl said," writes David Grossman, "But what if you stop willing it? What if you can't be bothered to have the will anymore?"[67]

※

We must keep the will and the dream alive. That is the work of faith.

This war will not end until everyone affected by the war dies. This will be in a very long time. And then it will live on in the inheritance of stories.

※

There will come a day when the war no longer lives in any people.

It will then live only on the page.

※

There will come a time when we, too, will live only on a page. A registry of birth. A registry of death.

※

A siren goes off in the airport. *Zman emet. Zman emet.* This is not a test. It is a real alarm, the robotic voice shouts. But the words translate as "This is a time of truth."

※

We spend Shabbat with my mother-in-law. She is confused but grateful. We push her wheelchair outside to see the carpet of trees on the hills all around. My mind is forested by turmoil. She places a frail hand on each of our heads and recites the Friday night priestly blessing. In our family, we also recite it before a child takes leave to travel. We are traveling. Soon, she, too, will travel. "May God bless you and protect you. May God be kind and gracious to you. May God bestow His favor upon you and grant you peace" (Num. 6:24–26).

They will be the last words she ever says to me.

⁂

I dream about hugging my grandchildren these many weeks. I can almost smell their sweaty necks when they sleep. They are completely innocent of all things related to war. Their simple exuberance will relieve my flatness. It will let me escape the war for a few minutes.

Grandchildren are my *nechama*, the consolation of all consolations. This is continuity. This is my joy and my faith in the future.

⁂

Barukh Dayan HaEmet. Blessed is the Judge. After a few months of pain and fear, my mother-in-law passes away into a peace not available to her people right now. Let her memory be for a blessing. May we remember her and not only the war time of her death.

⁂

Her funeral is delayed. First there is a military funeral of a nineteen-year-old soldier, Lavi Ghasi. Thousands have come and are congregating. They do not want to leave. My mother-in-law must wait in line. Hers was a long life of blessing. Her death is sad but not tragically so. It was a life to be celebrated. His was a life of service cut catastrophically short.

Morning Has Broken

The delay and the traffic irritate some people who turn around and go home. There are things to do. Who has time?

✿

Someone attends the shiva and says what a relief it is to go to the funeral of an old person.

✿

Don't despair. Despair is a black hole. It is hard to climb out once you fall in.

✿

"Despair leads nowhere," David Ben-Gurion warns. "Throughout the millennia of persecution, the Jews have realized this and never lost conviction in ultimate justice, peace, human equality. I am sure that the Jewish people have hard days ahead of them in Israel. They have overwhelmingly difficult tasks to accomplish and black moments to face. But having had the privilege of seeing what they can do when confronting the apparently impossible, I have total confidence in their ability to pass through the shadows and emerge unshaken, present in the land they have struggled so hard and suffered so greatly to regain."[68]

✿

Routine is the life-raft against despair. During the first weeks of the war, I heard the word, *shigra* (routine), over and over again. We were all holding on to an inch of that life raft together across the vast ocean. The routine will save us. We will not let the war rob us of our daily discipline.

Maybe the routine can save us, but I've lost mine. My routine is now worrying, checking my phone, thinking of what else I can or should do, feeling helpless, feeling helpful, praying for productivity. War has changed my center of gravity.

The Hebrew infinitive, *leshager*, also means to launch a rocket.

※

If the first Prime Minister of Israel tells us it will be hard but we must not despair, we must not despair. He is confident in us. This is the same man who came to the country in 1908 and walked the land. He said of those early days when so much of it was empty, "I knew our labour would prevail and that one day the country would be ours."[69]

※

Despair is a hurdle to dreaming.

Despair is a hurdle to being.

Touchdown

On the 365th day of this war, we will look back to its beginnings and trace its fateful trajectory. One entire year. I go all the way back to a memory in its earliest days for strength. My plane touched down in Ben Gurion Airport in the early evening, and the small, oval windows showed nothing but the indigo of a late October sky.

We were landing in the darkness of uncertainty on the twenty-second day of this brutal war.

When the wheels touched the runway, passengers clapped in relief.

The pilot with his pilot-y voice said in stilted English, "Welcome to Israel. Welcome home."

But in Hebrew, he added, *"Ein lanu eretz acheret."* We have no other country.

As the war continues day after difficult day, I replay the pilot's voice during that first landing in Israel. Remember this. Remember this always I tell myself. We have no other country.

The Soil

I travel with a group of students and faculty to Israel in January. We arrive at night, sleep a few hours, wake up early, pray and study, then take a bus to an urban farm whose workers are now on reserve duty. Next to tall glass towers in the friendly sun of a beautiful morning, we pick thousands of beets. We listen to Israeli music or sing.

Within the hour, we've split into smaller groups. Some of us develop our own simplistic farming methods. In my cluster, we turn the yellow crates over, sit on them, and use the sharp knives to quickly cut off the tops and place the beets in containers. Not too big. Not too small.

For those few hours, we are at home in the dirt, holding the land of Israel in our hands. It's the same soil made of decomposing mountains and rocks maybe as old as our forefathers and matriarchs, who planted and harvested, who dug wells and walked the land with their sheep. But now there is a sleek office building a hundred feet away where the sun's mid-day rays bounce off the glass.

۶

We supervise after-school activities with evacuee children from Sderot in Jerusalem. Kickball. Volleyball. Baking. Dancing. Coloring. Painting.

For a few minutes, they jump for a ball or run away in a game of tag. In Jerusalem, outside the old library at Givat Ram, they are breathless and laughing with strangers. The body that runs and hides also jumps with freedom.

※

The library where great scholars of the Bible, Talmud and Zohar did their research is now empty of books. The books have moved to a new beautiful National Library. For now, the room is filled with small children who know nothing of esoteric research. They display 8 x 11 sheets of white paper covered with their drawings.

Everything that seems permanent moves and changes places. Books. Buildings. Towns.

Later, we will go to Sderot to see how those children lived just a few months ago. We will stop at the sandy lot where the Sderot police station stood until it was overrun by Hamas and then bombed by the IDF. We visit the yeshiva that is rocket-proof so that its dedicated students do not have to leave their holy books for a minute. The roof has a large menora made of old Kassam rockets.

※

Mrs. Guri steps on to our bus late Thursday night as we are about to pull out of Ofakim. She is petite and wears a peach-colored beret and a party dress. She wishes us well and thanks us for coming. It means a great deal to her. She blesses the students in their studies with a joyous future. They should find jobs and spouses and be granted every good thing. It is a send-off one might expect to give guests who have traveled far for a family event.

What she does not say is that her two sons, Ariel and Ro'i, had all of those things but now are no longer alive to enjoy them. On October 7th, those two brave men rushed from their homes and saw terrorists in black approaching. They were shot and killed along with fifty-three other residents.

Mrs. Guri wanted to dedicate a Torah in their honor. A special man, who made it his mission to create little sparks of happiness everywhere for those who have suffered terrible losses, made it happen. Blessed friends with huge hearts sponsored the event. They all enter the circle with the Guri family to fortify them with strength. The whole town mourns and celebrates under a big white tent. We weep. We close our eyes. We eat.

The *sofer*, the scribe, helps students and residents write the Torah's last letters. Ariel and Ro'i become letters in a scroll. "This is the Torah: the voice of heaven as it is heard on earth, the word that lights up the world."[70] The Torah is complete. It is closed and dressed in its ornate silver case. It has been written with the blood of the living as a sign of respect for the dead. The new parchment will soften and darken slightly over time. The letters will be checked periodically. The Torah, if cared for properly, will be used for hundreds of years, and it will still honor Ariel and Ro'i and this awful time in history.

We dance the Torah through the streets of Ofakim until we reach the place where each young man was killed. Students wear Israeli flags like capes. Zionism is their superpower. We visit Ariel and Ro'i with this Torah. And then we dance the Torah to the yeshiva where they studied. May they continue to live in the words and in the dance.

A Feather of Hope

My X-ray technician was a middle-aged Black man who wore a large silver cross. He asked me to take off my dog tag; it was metal and too long for the machine. "We're twins," he said, "I've got the same one." He took the same dog tag out of his zippered jacket; it dangled right under his cross.

"I'm with you." He told me he confuses Christian patients with his jewelry. He doesn't care. They just don't understand him. "Man, I just want peace in the world."

Then we go back to the task at hand. The X-ray. "You can keep your shoes on. This will take less than five minutes." Maybe he will see through my heart and diagnose me with sorrow.

⁂

My childhood friend and I speak on Friday morning. She says it's raining in her Jerusalem suburb. It's the rainy season. Rain is good for Israel, but it's bad for war. "There was a sudden clap of thunder," she said, "and I stopped and thought: Is that thunder or an explosive?"

⁂

Good news on day #124 of the war: the Kinneret rose two inches because of rainfall.

❧

A Christian friend, a sweet religious man, is worried that I am despondent. Like me, he is puzzled by the intensity of hate toward the Jews. "So what is happening? Have we lost our way?"

He turns to sacred texts to find answers: "I search Job, Lamentations, the Psalms – indeed all of scripture – and I just cannot get my mind around why the Lord, throughout history, has seemingly deserted his chosen people on a regular basis."

"I believe we were created to love God and to love each other and have been given the great gift of creativity, but I am overwhelmed by the hate I see on a daily basis and have no answer. I am getting old (78), and all I can do is keep plugging along in my little corner."

"I wish you well," he writes at the end of his email.

I wish you well. And I wish you long, long life. And I wish there were more people like you, my friend.

❧

A student queries why we have changed the syllabus this semester. Why have we added antisemitism when there are other, important topics to study? Some people don't like change. No one likes antisemitism (except the antisemites). It seems odd to have to explain this. "The first task of love, its most urgent charge, is safety. I want my people to be safe."[71]

The first and primary job of any parent, leader, teacher, boss is to protect the flock, I tell them. The custody and safekeeping of others is a fundamental concern without which no other higher-order thinking is possible. Antisemitism is not just something we experience that wanes or intensifies with global trends. It has a history and a language that we must study. It aids in vigilance.

We role-play interactions of hate to prepare. There's the colleague, the casual antisemite, who drops a line at a party or the conspiracy theorist who believes that Jews masterminded 9/11 for their own ends. The conversation will be different still with the storekeeper who whispers to the clerk, "Don't let them jew you down." The scenes change, but the hate lingers.

※

The sign on a black metal fence says "Pain is Temporary. 154 Days is Unbearable." More than twice as many days pass. The sign is still up. It is, all of it, even more unbearable. We are running out of time.

※

I feared the hour would come. It came. Day #163 of the war. "It is with immense pain and deep sadness that I share with you that the Perez family were informed this evening that Captain Daniel Perez, twenty-two years old, has been declared as a fallen soldier captured by a terror organization."

The family heard the news on the 7th of Adar, the day that according to tradition Moses was born, and the day that he died. "No one knows his burial place to this day" (Deut. 34:6). Daniel, how many times did your Hebrew name appear in my prayers? It was so embedded in my brain that even after your death, I kept saying it.

We sat in your living room as your father told us proudly how you rushed to the Gaza border on October 7th and then he traced the tracks of where your tank had been on a laminated map. There was so much optimism in your father's voice, as if at any minute you'd walk through that door and fold into his arms. And into the arms of your mother.

❧

They knew that the DNA sample of blood in the tank was yours. You'd been injured, but other hostages were injured and lived.

You died that first day, like Itay Chen, who was also in your tank. But no one who loved or cared about you had any idea. Our hope lasted 163 long days and nights. We kept on hoping as if hope alone could lift and carry you home. We hoped in our ignorance because hope, like faith, sustains us when we know nothing and choose to imagine the best, even when we suspect the worst.

❧

"'Hope' is the thing with feathers," wrote Emily Dickenson, "That perches in the soul / And sings the tune without the words / And never stops at all."[72] The famous, quirky poet was wrong. Hope stops where knowledge starts. When you know someone is dead, hope shrinks and evaporates in an instant. It makes a fast exit, like a feather in a strong wind.

❧

"Officer" Daniel Perez was changed to "Captain." When an IDF soldier is killed, he automatically gets a raise in rank.

❧

An Uber driver named Iyob picked me up. His name must be Arabic for Iyov, in Hebrew and Job, in English. Seemed like Job was an appropriate name for the first person I met the day I learned that Daniel had died. Iyob heard me speaking Daniel's name and heard my misery as I spoke on the phone.

There was traffic. If I didn't get to the station, I'd miss the train. But, then again, what does it matter if I miss a train when a beautiful young person dies? The dead will forever be late.

Morning Has Broken

☙

A rabbinic colleague leaves a message of consolation on my phone. I call back and ask him about the Talmudic notion of *tefillat shav*, a useless prayer that seems senseless and goes unanswered because it goes against reality. Were the months of prayer for Daniel wasted because he was not alive the entire time?

No. He shares a teaching from Rabbi Jacob ben Wolf Kranz, the Maggid of Dubno (1741–1804) that has comforted him. Maybe it will comfort me. There really is no such thing as a *tefillat shav*, a wasted prayer, because although what one prays for may not come to fruition or the outcome is undesired, those prayers will always exist in the world for generations to come.

Think of it: Millions of unanswered prayers are in some storage facility somewhere making the world more virtuous and good by virtue of their existence.

These once-uttered prayers will be feathers of hope, light and buoyant, floating upward in the breeze.

☙

This colleague has spent a great deal of time with hostages and their families. He, too, is unsure how to pray now.

What should we pray for in such circumstances? Would death be preferable to warped lives in captivity?

No. A doctor I read about who prayed before seeing every patient was unsure what to say when he felt the greater mercy was death. Finally, he settled on five words: Let Thy will be done.

No. When my grandparents left their concentration camps and my mother her orphanage after the Holocaust, we could have asked the same question. Is a haunted, traumatized life worth it? As a granddaughter, I say yes. As a daughter, I say yes. Yes. Yes. They did laugh again. They cried plenty. But they also laughed a great deal.

Waiting

We've waited for hostages to be released. We've waited for the war to end. We've waited for those we loved to return from battle. We wait for good news – or at least not terrible news. And then there's the greatest wait of all: waiting for danger to strike. Iran threatens retaliation for the death of terror architect Ismail Haniyeh and other Hamas senior leadership and then does not retaliate. The streets whisper, "It will definitely happen tonight."

But it does not happen.

"It will definitely happen in the middle of Friday night. They always strike on Shabbat." Late Friday afternoon, I lie on a hotel bed in Jerusalem, in a room the color of turmeric, as my heart races. For over 300 days, I have felt belonging. I have felt proud and determined and, when I am honest, also beset by sadness, melancholy, guilt, regret, and hopelessness. But my heart has not raced. None of those uncomfortable feelings are as uncomfortable as this existential threat. Suddenly it feels like someone very heavy is sitting on my chest and squeezing my heart. Is it a heart attack? It could be a panic attack. I don't recognize these symptoms.

Saturday night arrives. The retaliation we've waited for still does not happen. Each day there is a reason it will happen on that day. And still it does not happen. The tension piles up and strains routines. People go out to do something normal before the not normal days begin.

※

There are three kinds of waiting. There is happy anticipation. Something good is about to happen, maybe on a particular day. We wait with eagerness. We wait patiently but more often impatiently for that day. We count. We distract ourselves. We develop rituals to help us manage the nervousness that we thinly veil as we pass the hours knowing that one day soon, we will be more joyful, more liberated, or more content. Very soon. Just not now.

※

There is waiting that is sheer boredom – waiting for a bus to arrive or a plane to leave. We sit in bland waiting rooms with old magazines at the dentist or the department of motor vehicles or even in cyberspace; these are spaces designed just for waiting so that we can traverse a passage of time that has no inherent meaning and demands nothing from us but patience. If the wait is short, we barely notice. If the wait is long, we fidget, then complain, then claim to lose our minds; then it all disappears instantly when the plane arrives, or someone calls our name.

※

Then there is the long wait of confusion when we do not necessarily know when the current situation will change or if the change will make it worse. The end of the wait might transform our lives. We wait in hospital waiting rooms for the inevitable news of death that still takes us by surprise. We wait for promotions. We wait to be loved. We wait for someone to notice us. We wait and wait for the messiah, and though the messiah tarries, we will wait longer. Jews have become experts at waiting.

We wait to see when the hostages will be rescued or released, and it is the longest wait I can remember in my lifetime.

Our Library

At the time of my first visit, there were only 115 chairs left on the ground floor of Israel's National Library in Jerusalem. Each chair had a photo of a hostage and a Hebrew book selected especially for that hostage: "Every person," the introduction to the exhibit states, "is a world unto themselves. A book awaits each of the hostages."

☙

The library reading rooms are crowded. I cannot find a seat. Scholars with curly sidelocks sit beside university students wearing hijabs. They are all secure here reading together as if whatever happened outside the library's walls had little to do with the pages in front of them.

☙

Some books on the empty hostage seats were selected by relatives or friends. Some reflected the hobbies or interests of the hostage. "We await their safe return, so that they may all continue to read and write the story of their lives."

And there, beneath the photo of red-headed Ariel Bibas, is a Hebrew picture book "Mommy and Me." I gasp. "This story must have a happy ending." Must it?

Maybe a hopeful ending is still possible.

The Windsurfer

The air before Shabbat in Jerusalem was quiet and tense. My heart fluttered and pressed against the imaginary heavy stone that had been placed on it. Several senior Hamas and Hezbollah leaders had been assassinated that week of the war. Reprisals were expected. They were promised. We left the lights and the fan on in the protected room just in case. There was a run on groceries.

I woke up Shabbat morning, and my first thought was, "We're still here." I pushed away the covers, but the blanket of dread remained. That night, after Shabbat and our evening prayers were finished, we rushed to read the latest news.

The big headline: Israel had won its first gold medal in the Paris 2024 summer Olympics. The windsurfer stood triumphantly on his first-place pedestal and belted out *Hatikva*. The retaliation may be on Monday. That day there was "only" a stabbing in Holon instead. Two dead and several injured. But on the world stage of Olympic excellence, we were victors for the day.

A friend likens her weariness to hanging over the side ropes of a boxing match. There is blood all over, but the main fight is not over. And she is out of strength.

The Saddest Day

It is day #312, Tisha B'Av. All of tragic Jewish history collapses into this day of commemoration. Today the color of the day is black with streaks of fresh blood. There is a tense expectation that somehow the senior leadership in Tehran knows that this is a day of mourning for our people and has planned to strike hard. We wake up waiting. Again, nothing happens.

The night before, we sat on the floor and read Lamentations, and the words are so very real that a survivor of the slaughter in Kibbutz Nahal Oz, a kibbutz in the Gaza Envelope, in the north-west of the Negev, constructs her own *kinah*, an elaborate acrostic poem called "O How She Sat Alone" that laces actual verses with images from that awful, awful day as she experienced them.

> *O How She Sat Alone*
> Nir Oz, full of blood
> Sderot, was like a widow
> A city stunned, and who is faithful to her?
> *O How They Sat Alone*
> In the shelter room
> One family, and another,
> And another, and another one.
> *O How They Sat Alone.*[73]

❧

There are many, many modern renditions of these intricate medieval acrostics this year. Words pour out of people like summer sweat. There is something oddly comforting in the permission to grieve communally as Jews face these demons of hate century after century. Likely one of these *kinot* will be added to the prayer book decades from now, and it will have more pages as hate mounts.

❧

In the late afternoon, my synagogue shows a documentary. In it, teachers have lost students. Rabbis have lost sons. Mothers who are scholars send their children off to war as they dole out mercy to students. I cry freely. The day calls for it.

Thirty years ago, I was in a synagogue in London, and a man was asked to lead a *kinah* about the Holocaust. After reading the first line, he broke down in tears. "Rabbi, I can't continue. Let someone else recite this for the congregation."

The wise rabbi paused, "No. We'll wait. Should someone who has less feeling recite it?"

❧

After the film, the lights go back on in the social hall. With the fluorescent lights back on, we wipe away the tears and discuss what we saw. We stretch because we can. We are not cramped in a tank in Rafah, where the fast ended hours ago.

❧

The day after, I asked a friend how her fast went. "This year, Tisha B'Av was too meaningful."

In the Blink of an Eye

Hersh and every hostage should come home in the blink of an eye. I heard Rachel Goldberg say and text that dozens of times over the course of this war. "Redemption," one midrash states, "comes in the blink of an eye."[74] You close your eyes and something good happens before you open them. The blink of time is brief.

※

Twilight is a complex time in Jewish law. It is neither day nor night, so it carries, according to some sages, the legal status of both day and night. The rabbis of old asked a fundamental question: What is twilight? This feature of Talmud study is endearing and helpful in conversations on any complicated issue: delve into a topic then back out of it for a while to clarify the terms.

What is distinctive about twilight is its uncertainty. Does it contain both night and day such that it is technically both at the same time? In pondering this question, the sages must have stepped outside to have a look: twilight happens "when the sun sets, as long as the Eastern sky is still reddened by the light of the sun. The lower part of the sky is colorless, and the upper part has not yet lost its color."[75] Twilight begins when color is drained out of the sky.

How long should it take for the sky to transition from day to night? Rabbi Nehemya says it last as long as it takes a person to walk about a mile after the sun sets. Rabbi Yosei claims it happens in the blink of an eye. Night enters. Day leaves. It is impossible to calculate due to its brevity.

Redemption comes in the blink of an eye. So does desperation.

An Even Sadder Day

Hersh is dead. I cannot believe it. He is dead.

Hersh's funeral is in an hour. We blinked, and he was suddenly gone with five others. All the waiting, the praying, and the negotiating did not bring him home. We were up against beasts. It feels like all of our dashed hopes will be there, buried in that small hollow rectangle of earth that holds his casket.

On day #331 of this war, the bodies of six hostages recently shot in a tunnel in Rafah were identified in Abu Kabir, Israel's only forensic institute.

This afternoon, color drained from the sky as a mother and father stand alone among thousands. Mourners will howl.

Israeli protestors have taken to the streets again. They wear their fury like the flags draped over their shoulders. Tomorrow the country will stage a general strike. Nothing is allowed to continue. Grieving turns to anger in a flash of the morning news.

Only days ago, those six hostages, Hersh Goldberg-Polin, Eden Yerushalmi, Ori Danino, Alex Lobanov, Carmel Gat, and Almog Sarusi, were alive. They could have lived. The tragedy of possibility is deadening.

❧

Hersh died on one of the closing days of summer when we typically try to bottle up the last hours of free time under a hot sun.

❧

His father tells us how before October 7th Hersh tried to make the world better and that after October 7th his face became a global symbol of freedom.

That face. That face.

❧

His mother asks, "What did I do to deserve him?" She apologizes to him if there was anything she could have done but did not do to obtain his freedom. She petitions him to intervene in the heavens and do all he can to make the world better from on high. With her other-worldly, ethereal voice, she begs that he finally be free. She asks for his help to survive.

❧

Two hundred fifty-one hostages were abducted on October 7th. One hundred and five were released in November in a hostage deal. Four were released before that. Eight hostages, to date, have been rescued alive. Thirty-seven dead hostages have been recovered and returned to Israel, including the six who will now be buried, and the three mistakenly shot by the IDF who were trying to escape. Thirty-three more hostages are not alive as confirmed by evidence.

❧

The phone keeps ringing. I don't want to talk to anyone. I just want to hug Rachel and say I'm sorry to Jon. They did everything they could for their boy. But we should have done more. We should have done more.

Morning Has Broken

❦

The president of Israel asked for forgiveness from the hostages' families.

❦

Hersh will lie in eternal rest in Jerusalem. But Jon and Rachel will never rest. If a day can get sadder than Tisha B'Av, it is a day on which the reality of terror is not in an acrostic.

❦

Another morning has broken. It has robbed us of our children.

Stop Hiding

That face. That face.

⁂

"*I will hide My face from them, and I will see what their end shall be*" (Deut. 32:20).

⁂

God, please do not hide Your face. It has been hidden too much over the past century. If You show it more, people will embrace faith. I know. I know. You show it every morning when the sun rises. But the skeptics need more. There are a lot of skeptics. Within each of us lives a skeptic.

⁂

For all these days, we've worried, loved, and honored the face of every hostage. Their faces appear on walls and fences and telephone poles. We have become familiar with their faces. But Your face is cloaked.

⁂

Rabbi Eliezer Berkovits attempted to explain how one could have faith after the Holocaust. The theological question is not inherently different for the unjust death of one than the death of millions. It is merely more stark. The number of times it is unjust is multiplied endlessly.

Rabbi Berkovits writes, "If man is to be, God Himself must respect his freedom of decision. If, man is to act on his own responsibility, without being continually overawed by divine supremacy, God must absent Himself from history."[76]

We wish to be awed at times like this, when we are given total freedom and autonomy to act. "But man left to his freedom," Rabbi Berkovits warns us, may put himself and others in jeopardy. "His performance in history gives little reassurance that he can survive in freedom. God took a risk with man, and He cannot divest Himself of responsibility for man. If man is not to perish at the hand of man, if the ultimate destiny of man is not to be left to the chance that man will never make the fatal decision, God must... be present in history."[77]

God must, according to Rabbi Berkovits, be "absent and present concurrently." He hides but cannot, in his absence, be "hopelessly inaccessible."

"Because of the necessity of his absence, there is the 'Hiding of the Face' and suffering of the innocent; because of the necessity of His presence, evil will not ultimately triumph; because of it, there is hope for man."[78]

❧

Faith in humanity may be harder to find right now than faith in God. Please do not be hopelessly inaccessible. I will keep looking.

❧

After tragedy, I ask where God is. But I don't ask where God is after encountering beauty or goodness or undeserved blessings. God is there, too. Maybe even more of God is there.

Praying in a Ruin

Since October 7th, I've been praying in a ruin. The prayer is not always prayer. The ruin is not always a ruin.

The prayer can be the way I speak to or about our broken world. The prayer can be the sharp and wordless inhale before checking the news or the teardrop that makes an almost visible line down my cheek.

The ruin is not always a building. The ruin is broken faith after that horrible day. It's the twisted faith in our security. It's our shattered faith in the unity of our people when we all came together then fell apart. It's our complicated faith in the relationship between Israeli and Diaspora Jewry. It's our challenged faith in Israel's allies. It's our questioning faith in democracy and in the allegiance of the rest of the world to a Jewish state. It's our tortured faith in politicians when another hostage is confirmed dead, and another poster is taken down.

꧂

Sometimes I have to stand in the ruin to speak to God because the place mirrors my internal ruin. If I am not true to myself, I cannot pray at all. God, I bring you the ruin of me. Even that I do not hide. Do not hide from me.

Morning Has Broken

❧

Another modern/medieval "Lamentation for a Beloved Land" is written by Liora Eilon, a survivor from Kibbutz Kfar Azza.

❧

> O How your dwellings have been *turned into ruins,*
> Your people become exiles in their own land?...
> O How your kibbutzim were destroyed, cities made desolate,
> Your people dead, your fields wasting away.
> Furrows ravaged, become fields of horror,
> All eyes devastated, dried out of tears.
> Your sons, daughters butchered undefended,
> Fair maidens hauled into captivity.
> And the plotters standing before them
> Whispering, rustling, and the land was silent.[79]

❧

Cities are desolate. Families are inconsolable. Dwellings turn into ruins.

❧

I am not alone in this ruin. There are many, many people who cannot erase the mental image of a burnt house and a charred baby. When I pray, my words cannot rebuild anything. The words tremble across the shards; they are unable to jump high or dance.

❧

I speak to friends whose children are serving in Gaza and on the edges of Lebanon. Many tell their parents nothing about what they've seen and heard or what it's like sleeping in empty Palestinian homes amidst someone else's things. These parents are angry that their twenty-year-old daughters and reservist sons have been called up again. They wonder where God is and why their prayers go unanswered and when hostages will come home as the clock ticks.

※

Like a ruin, there are layers upon layers to excavate. A ruin is the disintegration of something but not its total collapse. The partial existence of a ruin signals its outline and invites us to fill in the mystery of the missing space. This requires vision and patience. It is tough to have patience in wartime.

※

My faith has never been stronger. My faith has never been weaker.

※

"I was once walking along the road," said the Talmudic sage Rabbi Yosei, "when I entered the ruins of an old, abandoned building among the ruins of Jerusalem in order to pray."[80] A ruin is an odd place to pray. Rabbi Yosei sought out the silence of a ruin for its privacy. Perhaps he felt in some inchoate way that the ghosts of the place could serve as intercessors for his supplications.

Abandoned structures fascinate us. If they were destroyed to their foundations and erased by time, the intrigue is lost. Once they are rebuilt or repurposed, their appeal also fades. Buildings we passed hundreds of times we cannot conjure in our minds once they've been knocked down. A ruin is a piece but not the whole that allows our imaginations to fill in the gaps, like the connect-the-dot puzzles of our childhoods.

In *How Ruins Acquire Aesthetic Value*, Tanya Whitehouse suggests that ruins invite contrasts and what she calls ambivalent contemplation; they are ominous yet inviting, symbols of destruction with the soft promise of regeneration, atavistic yet sublime.[81] Henry James once wrote, "To delight in the aspects of sentient ruin might appear a heartless pastime, and the pleasure, I confess, shows the note of perversity."[82]

☙

I grew up in a home filled with antiques. Visitors found my house charming and museum-like. I visited museums. I did not want to live in one. To me the word "antique" meant the hinges didn't open with ease; there were scratches on a table surface. When purchased, there might have been someone else's leftover detritus in a drawer. I had enough of these ruins. As a teenager, I asked my parents for brand-new white bedroom furniture in our beautiful Victorian always-falling-apart house. The dresser's white textured panels were high gloss; its handles bright chrome. Everything about the drawers, desk, and night-table screamed NEW. I was the first and only owner. There was nothing, not even dust, in the drawers. No ghosts. No provenance.

My room looked incongruous, to be sure. I wanted it that way.

As an adult, however, I came to appreciate owning things that have a history, even if it's one I don't know. Someone else loved and cared for something enough that it lasted for decades or generations in our disposable world.

☙

Inside the ruin, Rabbi Yosei met the enigmatic prophet Elijah, who guarded the entrance so that the rabbi could complete his prayer in safety. When Rabbi Yosei finished, Elijah questioned him: "My son, why did you enter this ruin?" Then Elijah chastised the rabbi. "You should have prayed on the road."

"I was unable to pray along the road because I was afraid to be interrupted by travelers." Travelers always have questions. They might be talkative and distract the rabbi from his concentration in prayer.

Elijah persisted. Rabbi Yosei should have said an abbreviated prayer, he chastised. The rabbi concluded from this encounter that one must not pray in a ruin. One must pray on the road and offer heavenly words quickly. People are not an interruption; their questions form the work of the spiritual guide. Maybe this is what the prophet wanted to teach the rabbi. People are your business. Pray at length later.

※

It is unclear what bothered Elijah so much. Maybe Rabbi Yosei's prayer was supposed to be fresh, new, and untroubled by ghosts, just like my white furniture. While Rabbi Yosei sought to avoid the distraction of travelers, he invited the presence of time travelers in his ruin. He may have raised the voices of the dead who lived before the destruction or those who watched the destruction. Keep moving, advised Elijah. Pray on the road. Pray quickly. Be with the living. Move away from the dead.

※

The strange meeting continues. Elijah asked Rabbi Yosei about the experience of praying in a ruin. "Whose voice did you hear in that ruin?" The prophet asked Rabbi Yosei to stay away but then to come close.

The scholar heard a divine voice, like an echo of that roar of the Holy One, cooing like a dove. The sound of the lion and the sound of the dove are completely different: harsh and dominant, sibilant and calming.

The heavenly voice said, "Woe to the children. Because of their sins I destroyed My house, burned My Temple, and exiled them among the nations." God mourns exile and human pain and the loss of the spiritual center that was the *Beit Hamikdash*, the holy Temple. This compound hurt is manifest in the murmurs that fill the ruin.

※

Elijah was taken up in whirlwind and never died. In the liminal space between heaven and earth, he has special access to God and humans.[83] It is twilight forever for Elijah. He graces us with his presence at the Passover Seder, comes to circumcisions, and resolves Talmudic disputes. Because of his this-worldly and other-worldly existence, Elijah was able to confirm what Rabbi Yosei heard. God, it turns out, cries three times a day, every day, in that ruin. God cries about the exile.

Elijah, it seems, was not protecting Rabbi Yosei from thieves or attackers, but from hearing God's voice mourn Israel's abandonment. The ruin is the physical symbol of a covenantal breakdown. Shoo. It is best for a scholar's faith to remain intact. Stick to the road.

⁂

Every occupant has a story that took place in that ruin. Every demon and apparition left an impression. The building's remains still stand as a testament to what once was. Elijah understood, and now Rabbi Yosei understands, that God's melancholy lingers in the ruins.

⁂

Since October 7th, Jews have been praying in the ruins: the ruins of kibbutzim in the South, the ruins of empty homes in the North, the ruined promises of hostage deals not completed, and the ruins of lives mourned, of limbs lost, of minds boggled by the insanity of war. There is the ruin of student safety because of antisemitism on college campuses. The ruins are the fraying of belief in the Israel Defense Forces as a result of October 7th, or in Israel's political leadership, or America's, or England's, or South Africa's. There is the ruin of the United Nations and the Hague. There is the moral decay that lives in some American college presidents. There is the root of those who hate Israel and pretend that anti-Zionism is not antisemitism. The ruins are the trauma that a family lives with whose child was shot on Route 232, the road down to the Nova Festival, and that of the combat unit on the border. So much has been damaged.

༄

During this war, soldiers prayed in the ruins of a synagogue in Gaza from the sixth century during the Byzantine period. It was unearthed in 1965. There is a mosaic of King David on the floor, one of the Bible's greatest warriors.

༄

There are other actual ruins: the rubble of schools, hospitals, and refugee camps in Khan Younis, Shujaiya, and Gaza City. One day in the future, Gaza, that scrim of desperation that's just twenty-five miles wide and six miles long, will be rebuilt – as will the Jewish settlements of the Gaza Envelope. And we will wonder why we allowed this wreckage to happen if we are eventually going to rebuild it all. This will not relieve the area of terrorists; they grow like hydras straight from the ruins. We cannot be pacifists in the face of terror if we are to protect life and democracy.[84] We cannot become murderers either. These are choiceless choices.

༄

A person, too, can become a ruin.

༄

The head of ZAKA (Disaster Victims Identification) in the Lachish region of Israel and one of its founders got a call on October 7th and rushed south from his home in Ashkelon. There were still terrorists embedded in the towns and kibbutzim. Yossi entered at his own risk. A little girl sobbed in a car where both her parents had been murdered. She needed a sign that Yossi was not a terrorist. He said the first line of *Shema*.

Over the course of the day, hundreds of bodies needed to be stored and identified. One hundred and eighty volunteers worked until 4:30 in the morning and honored the memory of 237 people who were killed. The initial work went on for days. Yossi did not return home for almost a week. He lost over twelve pounds. "When I got home, my family, they didn't want to look at me. Not my wife, not my children, not my grandchildren." He had hit the bottom of despair.[85]

Yossi's volunteers are shells of themselves. "They can't bear to go home, can't bear to live their lives as normal." Yossi gathered seventy of them to talk with them. He told them his own story of that day and how he thought the bodies were talking to him, telling him their stories. People nodded. They, too, had that experience.

※

Rabbi Yosei heard voices come out of the ruins. Yossi heard voices come out of the ruins. The body can also be a ruin.

※

Saving bodies out of purgatory made a ruin out of those who sought to sanctify the dead.

Getting Better to Get Worse

"Sometimes, in the trenches," wrote Pat Barker in his World War I novel *Regeneration*, "you get the sense of something ancient… It was as if all the other wars had distilled themselves into this war, and that made it something you almost can't challenge."[86]

This war is like so many wars and also unlike it. It is both new and incredibly old. Hundreds of beepers go off in Lebanon in an astonishing display of targeted violence against terrorists. If it happened in a movie, it wouldn't ring true. New technology holds ancient hatreds in the ruin of human life. Then eight soldiers die hours before Rosh HaShana, the Day of Judgment. I lack the strength to say the words of *Unetaneh Tokef*. Too many died by fire this year. A friend in Israel says that this Rosh HaShana when we say that repentance, prayer, and charity will change the evil decree, we must add in *mesirat nefesh*, self-sacrifice. There has been too much sacrifice, more than Abraham could have imagined when he stayed his hand on Mount Moriah.

※

In Barker's novel, a poet who is also a war hero refuses to fight. He cannot stand the senseless slaughter. He is overly familiar with war. As a result, he is deemed mentally unwell and sent by the army to see a brilliant psychologist. The psychologist's paradoxical objective is to heal soldiers from the mental wounds of war so that they can fight again.

The conflict between Israel and the Palestinians quiets down so that it can heat up again. Everyone "gets better" so that they can get worse. The savagery is at once justified and senseless.

⁂

We check the news that supports our positions. We listen to this channel or that, read this newspaper or that. We block other people's facts. We allow our own beliefs to crowd out compassion. "I don't know what I am, but I wouldn't want a faith that couldn't handle facts."[87]

⁂

Why are books on war important, asks Samuel Hynes in *On War and Writing*? Hynes does not mean the history of war, the tableau of dates or the battlegrounds of conflict. He means how we internalize war and how it shapes our individual and collective consciousness and frames our identities. Personal accounts of war are critical "because *war* is important, because it's always present in our world, dozens of wars being fought, somewhere right now."[88]

War is intense, demanding, fraught, consequential, and one of the great dramas of human life. Hynes claims that many accounts of war are only written years or even decades after they are lived because "you don't see a war when you're in it."[89]

It is unclear what will remain when the flags of surrender are reluctantly unfurled, and the negotiations begin for a true ceasefire. When we rebuild and reconstruct, we will do so on layers of brokenness. As the rubble is cleared, the physical and psychological costs of war will disclose themselves on the hearts and souls of those who fought and those who observed slowly and painstakingly; our memory "dawdles and delays."[90]

※

I have not lived in Israel for over twenty years. I am merely an observer. Here's what I've observed: Jewish identity in the Diaspora can no longer be detached and separated from what happens in Israel. Only the naïve ever believed that it could. For years, maybe longer, pundits and Jewish communal leaders bemoaned the distance in values, leadership, and identity between Israelis and Diaspora Jews.

To repair the situation, we sent the American, the French, the Anglos, and the Argentinian Jews to Israel. We sent high school students, and college students, honeymooners, and seniors so that they could assume their places in this, the great project of the Jewish people, no matter their age or life stage. They bought shawarma and shakshuka, and admired soldiers, and bought Star of David necklaces for relatives and wore fine red strings for luck. They went home and shared their photos and talked about how incredible those days were and then went on with their lives.

Trips change us, sometimes, but usually the inspiration disappears like a misplaced postcard after a few days or weeks.

※

Israel, too, sends its citizens abroad. More of them simply go on their own to escape, to see family, to enjoy, to shop, to meet Jews who are not like their Jews. Some seek understanding. Some seek the mall. They are not likely transformed. That is not their objective. By and large, their identities are not challenged by such encounters but thinly informed by them. These trips are supposed to bond an extended family, but sometimes all they do is highlight the inconsistencies and strains. I am a foreigner here. I am a foreigner there. The space between two countries is vast and unconquerable.

There are Israelis who believe that only those on the frontlines who are willing to pay the ultimate price can possibly understand them. There are Diaspora Jews who feel they lack agency to form their own Jewish identities because they will always be tied to Israel's body politic. But these distances can be interrogated and diminished. You don't have to love everyone in a family to be a family. But we can all probably love people more than we do.

Rabbi Kook, the first chief rabbi of Palestine who died in 1935, who sang the song of self, his people, and all of humanity could not help the love he felt.

༺

A. B. Yehoshua spoke about the garments of identity that Diaspora Jews put on and take off as easily as clothing. Israeli-ness is not a covering that can be quickly removed when necessary, he admonished those who make no sacrifices for the State. He was criticized for this description. He apologized and then said it again.

༺

Every Jew is more Jewish because of this war. Every Israeli is more Israeli in the world because of this war. The ocean shrinks.

༺

"Wars sometimes unite societies while they're being fought, but in the end, they change and divide them."[91] In the beginning of this war, there was a surfeit of Jewish unity, a tidal wave of solidarity. We were on the same side. A year later, the fissures are showing; the fabric is unraveling. Israelis grateful for duffle-loads of supplies at the beginning of the war are more circumspect. Where are the tourists now? Where is the long-distance love?

Many Israelis caught in their own war, know little of the arrows of antisemitism in the West. Some have little notion of the pain Diaspora Jews are carrying. Suffering has more than one address. The Suffering Olympics offers no medals.

※

I bumped into an acquaintance in Jerusalem's Old City who asked me why I am not living in Israel within a few minutes of conversation. He moved only a few years earlier. Not an hour later, this happens again with a bookseller. Their evangelism irritates me and also makes me love these relative strangers.

※

We cannot get better to get worse. The mammoth divide that has separated us as a people inside and outside Israel should soften now. Our Jewish lives are dependent on each other.

※

We might actually heal during this war into one people, broken in some places, whole in others.

Sorry, Not Sorry

Usually, in the Hebrew month of Elul, as the Days of Awe get closer, my annual spiritual inventory begins, and the list of my wrongdoing lengthens. I hurt this one. I ignored that one. I lied to myself. I did not support this one. I insulted that one. I spoke ill of that one. I did not study enough. My prayer was unimaginative. I ate badly. I owe so many apologies.

But this Elul is different. My inventory contains a long list of apologies that others owe me. Hamas must say sorry. Hezbollah must say sorry. The UN must say sorry. The Hague must say sorry. People in encampments must say sorry. College presidents must say sorry. Whole countries must say sorry. Irresponsible leaders must say sorry. Antisemites everywhere must say sorry. The friends, neighbors, and colleagues who said nothing must also say sorry.

There are so many apologies owed that they crowd out my own. There is less room for introspection in my brain right now because it is filled with anger and pain. Repentance will have to wait until the fires die down.

I try to remember where I was this time last year – physically, emotionally, and mentally. My mind draws a blank. It's as if the clock started ticking on October 7th. Time has melted like the clockfaces in a Salvador Dali painting.

⁂

There is a Talmudic argument that debates the use of a straight or curly shofar on the High Holidays.[92] Should we use a straight shofar from an ibex to indicate our own rectitude on Rosh Hashana and then switch to the ram's curved horn on Yom Kippur when we are bent into submission and made crooked by our sins or the reverse?

The shofar, whose plaintive call mirrors our staccato cries of sin and pain, is regarded in this dispute as a visual symbol rather than as a primitive musical instrument alone. In Jewish law, however, we use the same shofar for both days. It is the ram's horn that Abraham blew when God stayed his hand at Isaac's binding, his raw cry of relief echoed down Mount Moriah.

This year, I will not close my eyes as the shofar is blown. I will stare at the shofar, bent and warped, as a mirror of my own mind.

⁂

"My heart will not retreat from any of the grief that exists in the world," wrote Rabbi Kook, "for I know that in this [grief] there is some revelation of the deficiency of the soul in all of its levels, whether as an individual, or as it relates to the collective." Grief helps us situate the pain, the knob of stubbornness, the knot of resistance that repentance will liberate us from but only if we lean hard into the grief.

The surface expressions of wrongdoing that I harp on and over which I beat my chest are only symptoms of root causes. Rabbi Kook does not let me bypass the grief. He asks me to bring deed, intellect, thought and imagination to grief's narrowness and find the expanse of love on the other side. Anger and grief are reactions to the same sorrow. One is outward. One is inward. The narrowness will open, Rabbi Kook tells me, if I let it: "And all the ways are wide open, for the lovingkindness of God is very great."[93]

༄

The Jewish mystic reminds me of the Sufi mystic Rumi. In his poem "The Guesthouse," Rumi tells me to invite in all of my uncomfortable feelings and let them stay a while.

> This being human is a guest house.
> Every morning a new arrival.
>
> A joy, a depression, a meanness,
> some momentary awareness comes
> as an unexpected visitor.
>
> Welcome and entertain them all!
> Even if they're a crowd of sorrows,
> who violently sweep your house
> empty of its furniture,
> still, treat each guest honorably.
> He may be clearing you out
> for some new delight.
>
> The dark thought, the shame, the malice,
> meet them at the door laughing,
> and invite them in.
>
> Be grateful for whoever comes,
> because each has been sent
> as a guide from beyond.[94]

༄

The war has made this emotional guesthouse larger than my real house. All the dark thoughts have crossed the threshold and seated themselves. I shudder to think of the dark thoughts of those who locked themselves in safe rooms and don't even have a home for the bad thoughts to enter. These dark clouds are not leaving for the foreseeable future. God, give me the wisdom to interrogate every scrap of exasperation and tendril of wrath so that the grieving can begin in earnest.

※

Then my two mystics meet the rationalist Maimonides. For now, I will call him the accountant. In his "Laws of Repentance," Maimonides acknowledges that "every person has sins and merits. One whose sins outweigh his piety faces dire consequences. One whose piety outweighs his sins is righteous, and the rest of us live in the balance. We hope to tip the scales in our favor. But we also don't know the weight of each action. That is only, Maimonides assures us, calculated by the real Accountant: "The accounting of sins and merits is carried out according to the wisdom of the Knowing God." The Accountant does not only measure individuals. The Accountant also puts countries and the whole world on the scale, Maimonides writes, and uses an accounting system that is beyond the ken of any human being.[95] Maybe every sorry that I ask for from terror groups, countries and colleges represents an apology God will also exact. I will never know.

Why would Maimonides bait us like that, telling us there's a cosmic methodology which we cannot grasp but that we will be responsible for on the days of judgment?

I sit in the question for days. Maybe Maimonides wanted me to understand that I cannot vindicate myself and be judged separately from my country and my world because we are all on that scale together. It's a Venn diagram of human duty. I am also my country and my world. I am obligated to consider the cosmic significance of every thought and deed as if the very world depended on it. And because of that I cannot ask for an apology from all those who have disappointed me this year without the willingness to join the collective attempt to save ourselves from the worst of ourselves.

❧

I bow my head in submission.

Jesters

The year milestone since October 7th inches closer and then it is upon us. The war has not ended. Even when it ends, it will not end. It will live on in the ruin of stories and memories. Documenting its small and significant moments is the work of journalists. Their work will continue. After a year, mine is done. October 7th is not an arbitrary date to start, but it is an arbitrary date to stop. If the war continues on the ground, in the air, in our hearts, and in our heads, then any date seems arbitrary.

We have come together in tears. We will also come together in joy. Of this, I am sure. There will be a new morning. God "rolls the light away from before darkness, and darkness from before light." Sadly, it seems that sorrow and anger are better adhesives for Jewish unity.

※

All of the mysteries of these twelve months have made me turn to Elijah the prophet. We have become friends over this war. I find his curious appearance in stories oddly comforting, as if he might appear right before me and heal all wounds and rescue us from our abandonment. Just as he resolves Talmudic disputes, will he answer my questions: How will the war end? When will it end? Will every last hostage be released? When will we taste happiness again?

Morning Has Broken

In the Talmud, Rabbi Beroka often encountered Elijah in the marketplace, a bustling labyrinth of commerce, and not where you expect to find a rabbi and a prophet in conversation. You might expect them to meet in a sanctuary or a study hall. But no. They meet where there are diverse faces: the rich and the poor, the pious and the renegade, the local and the stranger. If you want to find God's word, go to the market.

On this occasion, Rabbi Beroka asked Elijah if there was anyone worthy at that very moment for life in the world-to-come.[96]

No.

In the meantime, the rabbi saw a stranger in the market who wore black shoes and did not wear ritual fringes. Jewish men at the time did not wear such shoes. Jewish men wore ritual fringes. The stranger stood out.

Elijah said, "That man is worthy of the world-to-come."

This was shocking to the rabbi, who, no doubt, expected a visibly righteous person to be singled out for this reward. He rushed to the man and asked, "What is your occupation?"

Rabbi Beroka believed that if you had the right job in this world, you'd have an all-access pass to the next.

The strange man in the black shoes told Rabbi Beroka to go away and come back the next day. The next day, Rabbi Beroka was bolder and asked the man what he did for a living and also why he wore those black shoes and did not wear fringes. It must have eaten at Rabbi Beroka that this man who did not even show basic respect for tradition would achieve its highest honor.

The man replied that he moved among Gentiles and did not want to be known as a Jew. He was a spy who sought information about government decrees that would negatively impact his people. He would then report them to the sages so that they could pray for mercy and an annulment of the decree.

Rabbi Beroka was not one of the sages privy to these secrets. The strange man with the black shoes also explained that he could not speak the day before because he had to pass on a critical piece of information. He prioritized his job over a conversation with a stranger in the marketplace.

❧

This exchange surely unsettled the rabbi, who entertained only one path of righteousness and now saw another. This man in the black shoes risked his life every day for his people. He did not engage in study or lengthy prayer. Whatever the world-to-come is, it might look like a market full of spirits with diverse faces and divergent paths.

As Rabbi Beroka and Elijah stood in the market, Elijah pointed out two others who would similarly be joining the man with the black shoes in the world-to-come. Not surprisingly, Rabbi Beroka made his way over and asked the same question: What is your occupation?

They said to him: "We are jesters, and we cheer up the depressed. And when we see two people who have a quarrel between them, we strive to make peace."

The comedians and the peace-makers have a place in the world-to-come. This does not mean that Rabbi Beroka is not in the world-to-come right now picking up spy tips and one-liners. But it must have expanded his picture of worthiness while also expanding ours.

❧

Imagine a world full of jesters and peace-makers to replace the crowd of haters and bullies, murderers, terrorists, extremists, and tormentors.

❧

I ask myself Rabbi Beroka's question: What is my occupation if it is not to make others laugh and bring them together in peace?

※

Whatever the world-to-come is, it is a place that privileges laughter. So much laughter. There may be a sky full of jesters up there just waiting for us. And what is faith but the capacity to hold God's hand and laugh out-loud at the smallest joy?

※

I pray that all of those who died on October 7th on that broken morning and in its aftermath are somewhere together, sitting in the tenderness of shared anguish and able to laugh – just a little – in each other's company.

※

Whatever it means to live in this world of utter pain and utter blessing, it is also a place of kindness, of justice, of service, of sacrifice, of peace, and of righteousness.

And of laughter.

Still.

Acknowledgments

To Rabbi Doron and Shelley Perez, and Jon and Rachel Goldberg-Polin: thank you for your friendship and for inspiring such hope in me and in so many others. You are the English voice of redemption, and you've each used that voice for the return of every hostage, even as you lost your own beautiful boys.

I am grateful to Elliot and Debbie Gibber who dedicated this book to the memory of all who gave their lives in this war and whose eggs say *Am Yisrael Chai*.

Thank you Matthew Miller, Rabbi Reuven Ziegler, Eliyahu Misgav, Tani Bayer, Ita Olesker, Alex Drucker, Tomi Mager, and all my good friends at Koren Publishers Jerusalem. Caryn Meltz has a saint's patience. You have done so much to put the books that matter most into our hands and into the hands of IDF soldiers. We are all telling this story together, but you are living it. May all your children stay safe and come home soon.

I am grateful to my friends and family who carry me over despair, and to the little people most of all: Erez, Adi, Amir, Lev, Ori, and Oren and those yet to be born. A shout-out to our Sefaria Word-by-Word writer's group and the support and encouragement they've given me over the past year. Special thanks to Terri and Andrew Herenstein, the blessed people who sponsored the Torah dedication for the Guri family described on these pages, and for their continued affection and support.

Thanks to my colleagues and students at Yeshiva University, especially all those associated with the Rabbi Lord Jonathan Sacks-Herenstein Center.

I extend my appreciation to the UJA-Federation of New York for sponsoring a trip for rabbis and educators a few weeks into the war. That visit began my journal of the war as an Israeli citizen and Jew of the Diaspora. Moving between the United States and Israel, I saw firsthand the travesty of the war and the thousand kindnesses that tumbled out of it. Good deeds will not bring back the dead, but they affirm our belief in the living.

Endnotes

1. Kiddushin 49b.
2. Proverbs 18:8.
3. Yoni Heilman, "Dairy of an IDF Solider, Part VII," *Sapir* (Jan. 18, 2024), https://sapirjournal.org/war-in-israel/2024/01/diary-of-an-idf-soldier-part-vii/
4. https://www.timesofisrael.com/liveblog_entry/jordans-october-7-restaurant-says-its-changing-name-due-to-political-pressure/
5. Bret Stephens, "Israel's Five Wars," *The New York Times* (July 30, 2024). https://www.nytimes.com/2024/07/30/opinion/israel.html
6. Nimrod Palmach, "A Soldier's Call to War on October 7," *The Jerusalem Post* (Jan. 9, 2024). https://www.jpost.com/opinion/article-781299
7. See Sota 48a, JT Ma'aser Sheni 5:5, JT Sota 9:11.
8. Rabbi Jonathan Sacks, *The Power of Ideas: Words of Faith and Wisdom* (Hodder Faith, 2023), 81.
9. David Bromwich, introduction, Hannah Arendt, *On Lying and Politics* (Library of America, 2022), xvii–xviii.
10. David Grossman, *Writing in the Dark: Essays on Literature and Politics* (Farrar, Straus, and Giroux, 2008), 60.
11. Daniel Gordis, *If A Place Can Make You Cry: Dispatches from an Anxious State* (Crown, 2002), 13.
12. Erica Brown, "Thanksgiving: This Year in Jerusalem," *The Times of Israel* (Nov. 22, 2023). https://blogs.timesofisrael.com/thanksgiving-this-year-in-jerusalem/
13. Rabbi Jonathan Sacks, "Chanukah in Hindsight," *Covenant and Conversation* (Dec. 19, 2019): https://rabbisacks.org/archive/chanukah-in-hindsight/.

14 Azriel of Gerona, *Sha'ar haKavvanah*. See Gershom Scholem, *Reishit ha-Qabbalah* (Schocken, 1948), 143–144. Translated by Daniel Matt, *The Essential Kabbalah* (Castle Books, 1983), 110.
15 Peggy Noonan, "Israel Needs a New Leader," *Wall Street Journal* (Nov. 2, 2023).
16 Natan Sharansky, *The Case for Democracy: The Power of Freedom to Overcome Tyranny and Terror* (Public Affairs, 2006), xxxiv.
17 Kwame Anthony Appiah, *Cosmopolitanism: Ethics in a World of Strangers* (W.W. Norton & Company, 2007), 31.
18 R. Samson Raphael Hirsch, *Chapters of the Fathers* (Feldheim Publishers, 1979), 70.
19 Jonathan Haidt, *The Righteous Mind: Why Good People are Divided by Politics and Religion* (Vintage, 2013), xxii–xxiii.
20 Todd May, *A Fragile Life: Accepting Our Vulnerability* (University of Chicago Press, 2017), 64.
21 Tekoa was also regarded as a city on the outskirts of Jerusalem that could provide an outer protective layer. See Jeremiah 6:1.
22 Shalom Freedman, *Life as Creation: A Jewish Way of Thinking About the World* (Jason Aaronson Inc, 1993), 39.
23 James Baldwin, *The Fire Next Time* (Vintage International, 1993), 55.
24 Ibid., 40.
25 *Orot HaKodesh* II, 444–445.
26 Adam Kirsch, "Campus Radicals and Leftist Groups Have Embraced the Idea of 'Settler Colonialism,'" *Wall Street Journal* (Oct. 26, 2023). https://www.wsj.com/world/middle-east/campus-radicals-and-leftist-groups-have-embraced-the-deadly-idea-of-settler-colonialism-b8e995be
27 https://tinyurl.com/y6twu633.
28 For several papers on the way in which numbers are manipulated to affect public policy and perception, see *Sex, Drugs and Body Counts: The Politics of Numbers in Global Crime and Conflict*, eds. Peter Andreas and Kelly M. Greenhill (Cornell University Press, 2010). For a review of the book, see Aaron G. Montgomery, "Review of *Sex, Drugs and Body Counts: The Politics of Numbers in Global Crime and Conflict*, edited by Peter Andreas and Kelly M. Greenhill." *Numeracy* 4, no. 1 (2011): Article 8. DOI: http://dx.doi.org/10.5038/1936-4660.4.1.8
29 Beverly Daniel Tatum, *Why Are All the Black Kids Sitting Together in the Cafeteria?* (Basic Books, 2003), 24.
30 Ibid.
31 Rachel Goldberg, "I Hope Someone Somewhere Is Being Kind to My Boy," *The New York Times* (October 12, 2023). https://www.nytimes.com/2023/10/12/opinion/israel-hamas-hostage.html

32 Isaac Bashevis Singer, https://www.nobelprize.org/prizes/literature/1978/singer/lecture/ (December 8, 1978). It is also available in print: *Nobel Lecture* (Farrar Straus & Giroux, 1979).
33 Rabbi A. J. Heschel, *The Prophets*, vol. I (Prince Press, 1999), 16.
34 Rabbi Joseph Soloveitchik, "Confrontation," *Tradition*, 6:2 (1964), 20.
35 Shabbat 31a.
36 This speech was given by Senator Kennedy to a Zionists of America convention, in the Statler Hilton Hotel, New York, NY on August 26, 1960, https://www.presidency.ucsb.edu/documents/speech-senator-john-f-kennedy-zionists-america-convention-statler-hilton-hotel-new-york-ny.
37 Rabbi Lord Jonathan Sacks, "Give Peace a Chance, Even If It Means Living with Differences," *The Times* (May 12, 2005).
38 Todd Gitlin, *Letters to a Young Activist* (Basic Books, 2012), 3.
39 Rachel Danziger Sharansky, "Forever Choosing Life," *Times of Israel* (Oct. 13, 2023).
40 Rabbi Joseph B. Soloveitchik, "The Symbolism of Blue and White," in *Man of Faith in the Modern World: Reflection of the Rav, Vol. II*, ed. Abraham R. Besdin (Ktav, 1989), 30.
41 Ibid., 31.
42 Ibid., 33.
43 *Ethics of the Fathers* 2:16.
44 Pete Davis, *Dedicated: The Case for Commitment in an Age of Infinite Browsing* (Avid Reader Press, 2022), 16.
45 Taanit 11a.
46 C. S. Lewis, *A Grief Observed* (HarperOne, 1994), 5.
47 https://en.wikipedia.org/wiki/Snack
48 Oliver Sacks, *Musicophelia: Tales of Music and the Brain* (Vintage, 2008), 44–45.
49 Daniel Gordis recounts this story in a footnote in *Impossible Takes Longer: 75 Years after Its Creation, Has Israel Fulfilled Its Founders' Dreams?* (Ecco, 2023), 44.
50 Maimonides, "Laws of Kings," *Mishneh Torah* 5:10.
51 Robert Frost, "Mending Wall," *Frost: Collected Poems, Prose & Plays* (Library of America, 1995), 39.
52 Clarrisa Ward, Brent Swails, and Rachel Clark, "First on CNN: Father Describes How His Young Daughter Emily Hand Survived Hamas Captivity," CNN (Nov. 28, 2023). https://www.cnn.com/2023/11/28/middleeast/thomas-hand-emily-hostage-intl/index.html.
53 "One Day," by Matisyahu.
54 Kieran Setiya, *Life is Hard* (Riverhead Books, 2022), 169.
55 I was relieved to read the same observation confirmed by a teacher and writer who has held up so many during this war, Shayna Goldberg, in her article

on abnormal/normal days: "It is a sign of resilience to be able to ponder your existence while sitting on the beach reading a book or sipping an ice coffee next to the pool," in the *Times of Israel* (Aug. 5, 2024). https://blogs.timesofisrael.com/feeling-grateful-for-what-might-be-our-last-normal-day/

56 Susan Sontag, *On Photography* (Picador, 2001), 15.
57 Ibid., 24.
58 A. B. Yehoshua, *Friendly Fire*, trans. Stuart Schoffman (Mariner, 2009), 338.
59 Amy Spiro, "Mother of Hostage Killed by Troops: 'I Wasn't Angry at the IDF for Even a Minute,'" *The Times of Israel* (December 25, 2023). https://www.timesofisrael.com/mother-of-hostage-killed-by-troops-i-wasnt-angry-at-the-idf-for-even-a-minute/
60 Deborah Lipstadt, *Golda Meir: Israel's Matriarch* (Yale University Press, 2023), 225.
61 Ibid.
62 Maimonides, "Laws of Repentance," *Mishneh Torah* 1:1.
63 Rena Quint with Barbara Sofer, *A Daughter of Many Mothers* (self-published in Israel, 2017), 11.
64 Ibid., 23.
65 Samantha Irby, *Quietly Hostile* (Vintage International, 2023).
66 https://www.urbandictionary.com/define.php?term=To+Jew.
67 David Grossman, *To the End of the Land* (Vintage International, 2010), 420.
68 David Ben-Gurion, *Memoirs* (The World Publishing Company, 1970), 156.
69 Ibid., 27.
70 Rabbi Jonathan Sacks, "Introduction," in *The Koren Shavuot Maḥzor* (Koren Publishers, 2016), lxxxi.
71 Leon Wieseltier, "Savagery and Solidarity," *Liberties*, 4:2 (Winter, 2024), 313.
72 *The Essential Emily Dickenson*, ed. Joyce Carol Oates (Ecco, 2016), 11.
73 Nurit Hirschfeld-Skupinsky, "O How She Sat Alone: A Lamentation," in Tamar Biala, ed., *Dirshuni: Contemporary Women's Midrash II* (forthcoming).
74 *Midrash Lekach Tov* on Esther 4:17.
75 Shabbat 34b.
76 Eliezer Berkovits, *Faith After the Holocaust* (Maggid, 2019), 110.
77 Ibid.
78 Ibid.
79 Liora Eilon, "Lamentation for a Beloved Land," in Tamar Biala, ed., *Dirshuni: Contemporary Women's Midrash II* (forthcoming).
80 This legend is recounted in Berakhot 3a.
81 Tanya Whitehouse, *How Ruins Acquire Aesthetic Value* (Palgrave, 2018), 2.
82 Henry James, *The Italian Hours* (Penguin Classics, 1995), 147.
83 For more on these Talmudic legends, see Daniel Matt, *Becoming Elijah: Prophet of Transformation* (Yale University Press, 2022), 50–89.

84 For a brief history of Jews and pacifism, see Shlomo M. Brody, *Ethics of Our Fighters: A Jewish on War and Morality* (Maggid, 2024), 3–18.
85 Yossi Landau, "This Is the Sanctity of Man," *One Day in October*, eds. Yair Agmon and Oriya Mevorach (Toby Press, 2024), 348.
86 Pat Barker, *Regeneration* (Plume, 2013), 83.
87 Ibid.
88 Samuel Hynes, *On War and Writing* (University of Chicago Press, 2018), 11.
89 Ibid., 21.
90 Ibid., 32.
91 Ibid., 34.
92 Rosh Hashana 26b.
93 Rabbi Abraham Isaac HaKohen Kook, *Hadarav: His Inner Chambers*, trans. Bezalel Naor (Maggid/Orot, 2024), 157.
94 Jalal al-Din Rumi, "The Guesthouse," *The Essential Rumi*, trans. Coleman Barks (HarperOne, 2004), 109.
95 Maimonides, "Laws of Repentance," *Mishneh Torah* 3:2.
96 Taanit 22a.

The fonts used in this book are from the Arno family

The Toby Press publishes fine writing
available at leading bookstores everywhere.
For more information, please visit www.tobypress.com